AGAINST
the
WALL

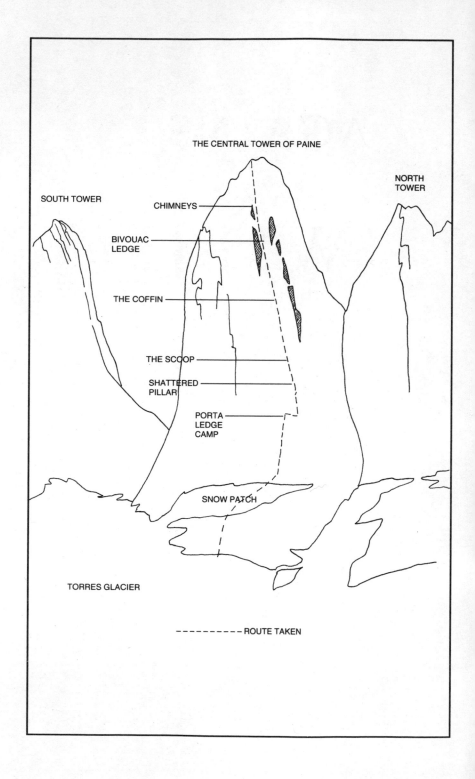

THE CENTRAL TOWER OF PAINE

NORTH TOWER

SOUTH TOWER

CHIMNEYS

BIVOUAC LEDGE

THE COFFIN

THE SCOOP

SHATTERED PILLAR

PORTA LEDGE CAMP

SNOW PATCH

TORRES GLACIER

-------- ROUTE TAKEN

AGAINST
the
WALL

Simon Yates

JONATHAN CAPE
LONDON

First published 1997

1 3 5 7 9 10 8 6 4 2

© Simon Yates 1997

Simon Yates has asserted his right
under the Copyright, Designs and Patents Act, 1988
to be identified as the author of this work

First published in the United Kingdom in 1997 by Jonathan Cape,
Random House, 20 Vauxhall Bridge Road, London SW1V 2SA

Random House Australia (Pty) Limited
20 Alfred Street, Milsons Point, Sydney,
New South Wales 2061, Australia

Random House New Zealand Limited
18 Poland Road, Glenfield,
Auckland 10, New Zealand

Random House South Africa (Pty) Limited
Endulin, 5A Jubilee Road, Parktown 2193, South Africa

Random House UK Limited Reg. No. 954009

A CIP catalogue record for this book
is available from the British Library

ISBN 0-224-03758-7

Typeset by MATS
Printed and bound in Great Britain by
Mackays of Chatham PLC

To my parents,
with love

Contents

But risk we must, because the greatest hazard
    in life is to risk nothing.
The man, the woman who risks nothing does nothing,
    has nothing, is nothing.

Anonymous

Jackie Simpson.

Introduction

This book follows the progress of a single mountaineering expedition to Chilean Patagonia. Although its objective – a new route on the Central Tower of Paine – was notable in pure climbing terms, that was not my main reason for choosing this particular story to tell as opposed to a dozen other climbs which, in their different ways, have been just as taxing. For more than ten years now, I have roamed the world's mountains, searching out new challenges. On many occasions I have returned home disappointed, my objectives unfulfilled. At other times, I have been more lucky and managed to complete some fine first ascents – the West Face of Siula Grande in Peru, Leyla Peak and Nemeka in Pakistan, to name a few – peaks all unknown to those outside mountaineering circles and many within. All these I hope have been a small contribution to the development of the sport.

At present there seems to be an unimaginative fashion for repeating the easiest existing routes on the world's fourteen highest peaks – those above 8000 metres. Is this the only way that individual climbers can gain public recognition? It could be argued that in the long term this trend offers no way forward for a sport whose progression has always relied on adventurers –

those willing to step into the unknown, to produce new, harder climbs that inspire others to even greater feats.

What made this adventure different from others was not just the savagery of the Patagonian weather, or spending such prolonged periods on a 4,000-foot vertical rockface, but the profound psychological changes I underwent at the time.

For me, the Patagonian expedition was a turning point, marking a very sudden shift in my attitudes to many things and the start of a new phase of my life. Perhaps this change was due to the extremity of the situations I experienced in Chile, or more simply a matter of timing, or maybe a combination of the two. Whatever the cause, my perspectives altered in a clear and precise way.

Later, when I thought about what had happened, I started drawing parallels with day-to-day life, seeing how sometimes, through laziness or neglect, we carry on with a course of action even though we know it could have potentially damaging consequences. I then began to think about how we come to decisions and their effect on our own well-being and that of those around us. In many ways, it all boiled down to a question of attitude.

So in short, this book is about attitudes. If, at times, I appear unduly critical of my friends, I can only apologise to them. I am equally critical of myself. I intended this account to be frank because there would be little point in setting down what took place internally as well as externally unless I am honest about what I observed and felt. If what I have written gives just a few people the courage to change, and to step back from the brink, then I have succeeded.

ONE

Up the Wall

I lay in a state of semi-consciousness, reluctant to wake fully, feeling secure in thick layers of clothing and a snug down sleeping bag. My body ached, but not unduly so. It felt like a Saturday morning and the deliberate oversleep that comes after a week of work and a satisfying Friday night in the pub. I had no idea where I was.

I tried to prolong the dozing, convinced that I deserved a lie-in, but my senses had other ideas. Wherever I was, it was windy. The sounds of flapping fabric rose and fell with each gust, and at times the noise reached a frenzied pitch as piercing draughts of icy air crossed my face. There was also a creaking sound and a distinct side to side swaying motion. Perhaps I was on a boat. No, more like a large ocean-going yacht, perhaps in the South Atlantic, hopping from island to island.

The dream didn't last long. I began to hear a hissing, faint at first, rising in intensity as I focussed on it. The sound was very familiar. It was snow, falling on to the nylon canopy above me. Suddenly I was wide awake. We could do without this, I thought, today of all days. I let out a long tortured groan.

Opening my eyes, I viewed my surroundings as if I'd not seen them before. I was lying on a piece of taught nylon fabric, six feet long and two feet wide. The stitched sleeves around the edge of the fabric contained an aluminium pole frame. I knew that the platform was hanging from a single point about ten feet above, suspended on six nylon webbing straps, one to each corner of the frame, the other two in the centre of the side poles. Outside the webbing straps was a thin nylon canopy. It was all that protected me from the storm. The whole structure resembled a camp bed, but instead of standing on collapsible legs it hung from above. Climbers call these hanging beds porta-ledges. They were invented by Americans who used them to scale the huge granite cliffs of Yosemite in California, so steep and smooth that they offered no natural ledges on which to sleep.

The storm continued unabated outside, making me reluctant to remove the canopy and face the day. By staying quiet and still, I reasoned, I wouldn't wake the others. Soon we would have to start the daily routine and melt snow for drinks. That could wait, though. I felt no sense of urgency. The storm outside was likely to have ruined our climbing plans for the day. I could relax for a few minutes more, safe and comfortable in my own small horizontal world.

Lying still, I contemplated our situation. About six feet above me in a double portaledge were my friends Noel Craine and Paul Pritchard, and to the side of them in another like mine lay Sean Smith. Our little commune was hanging from half a dozen metal pegs and bolts hammered and drilled into an almost vertical granite wall. More than a thousand feet beneath us lay the Torres Glacier. We were perhaps a third of the way up the eastern face of the Central Tower of Paine, with another 2,500 feet or so of vertical granite above us. The most difficult climbing was still to come. We had spent nine days, spread over two weeks, in appalling weather to get this far. It had taken a week of travelling from Britain to reach the mountain in a remote region of Chilean Patagonia at the southern tip of South America. Before that, there had been months of planning at home and, having put all our money into the trip, we would all return penniless.

When I thought about what we were doing in such cold, rational terms, it seemed rather pointless. It was certainly very abstract.

I had experienced these feelings before on previous expeditions. When the weather was good and the climbing going well, my spirits would soar. My optimism knew no bounds. It was possible to convince myself, quite unrealistically, that the climbing would be over in a matter of days. I imagined returning triumphantly from the summit and travelling into the nearest town to celebrate. Afterwards, we would be free to do another climb, lie on a beach or travel. Then, predictably, the bad weather would return, or some very difficult time-consuming climbing would be encountered, prompting more sober thought. At times, especially during prolonged storms, I would find it difficult to remain positive and make an effort to be outwardly confident, so as to avoid pulling others down and jeopardising the expedition's success. Others obviously had similar thoughts, producing a level of group confidence that sometimes was quite at odds with reality.

Outside my flimsy cocoon the storm was gathering force, the fierce Patagonian wind coming in violent bursts that lifted the portaledge away from the rockface. The swaying motion, combined with knowledge of the 1,000-foot drop below, made me feel uneasy. I knew that the anchors were not likely to pull out, but conditions were becoming uncomfortable. I wondered how much snow had already accumulated on the slabs beneath us, primed to avalanche. If a retreat proved necessary, which seemed likely, we would have to cross them. Although my sleeping bag had lost none of its warmth and security, I was finding it increasingly difficult to justify my laziness. The multitude of pathetic reasons for lingering – mostly centred on a wish to delay getting cold and wet – were being eroded by the minute.

It was Christmas Day. Back in England, all my family and friends would be up already, would have had a leisurely breakfast and opened their presents. Perhaps they had been out visiting, or were just lounging around, warm and comfortable in their homes. By now, the Christmas dinners would almost be ready, the tables set. Soon they would be sitting down to enormous meals. Maybe some were making their way back from the pub, already merry from a few lunchtime drinks. I envied them. It was only the start of our day, and it didn't look like being a good one.

I thought of all the miserable, non-event birthdays I had spent in the mountains, usually sitting in a tent on a rubble heap moraine. Occasionally they were marked in some small way; someone might bake a cake, or produce a novel meal. Mostly they passed unnoticed, just like any other day. The climbing always seemed more important. Because of the seasons and the distribution of the world's mountains, I had rarely been in camp for Christmas. The only other occasion I could recall was the previous year. I had been on an Anglo-Polish winter expedition on Nanga Parbat in the Pakistani Karakoram. It was bitterly cold. The presence of deep snow, combined with the Polish Catholics' spirit, spurred us to some sort of celebration. We even had a Christmas tree in the mess tent. It had been exceptional, but afterwards we were trapped in base camp by a week-long storm.

My portaledge began swinging again, this time not due to the wind. Noel and Paul were making a move. Our portaledges shared some of the same anchors, which transmitted their movement to me. I could hear their voices, but the background noise was too great to make out what they were saying. I would wait for their verdict on the weather; besides, there was still no sign of life from Sean.

After some delay, the familiar sound of a zip signalled that someone was going to brave the storm. I heard the outside world being greeted with a loud groan, which I recognised as Noel's. He yelled into the wind. 'And merry Christmas to you too!' His heavy sarcasm prompted a round of similar responses and signalled that Sean was awake.

Noel climbed down from above on to the small natural ledge beneath his portaledge and was now standing next to mine, so making it possible to talk to him without shouting.

'What's it like out there, Noel?'

'Awful. There's been a foot of snow in the night. I think we're going to have to climb down.'

Still in my sleeping bag, I loosened the drawcord and pulled up the canopy. Once exposed to the elements, it was difficult to see through the driving snow. I peered out at the bleak scene through watering, squinted eyes. Paul climbed down to join Noel and stood almost knee deep in fresh snow as Sean started to clamber out. There was a lot more snow than I expected, and it needed no second thoughts about getting down the mountain as fast as possible. Paul and Noel were already packing their rucsacs.

Back under the canopy, the storm was little more than a noisy distraction. Pulling on my jacket, I silently cursed myself for being lazy and not getting up earlier. Although I had dreaded leaving the warmth and comfort of my sleeping bag, I was out of it in an instant and hurriedly putting on my boots and gaiters. I removed the canopy again.

As usual, getting out of the portaledge proved tricky. They were fine to lie in, but once weight was placed unevenly on one side, they had a tendency to tip over. Noel had already experienced this instability the previous morning. In a rush to take a pee, the sudden tipping motion had caught him off guard and he had fallen. Fortunately we all slept in our climbing harnesses, tied to short lengths of rope from the anchors, and this had stopped him from plummeting a further 1,000 feet to the glacier. Nevertheless it had been an alarming start to his day.

Deeply aware of Noel's heart-stopping incident, I contorted my body to get my legs round the nylon webbing and created an unnerving rocking motion. Once it had stopped I gently lowered my feet over the edge before slithering down on to the ledge next to Noel.

Everyone was up now and frantically stuffing gear and clothing into rucsacs. Mine had filled with snow in the night. It produced a momentary white-out as I emptied it into the wind.

Without bodies to weigh them down the portaledges thrashed

around in the wind. I had visions of them being ripped from their anchors and soaring off across the Pampas. They were certainly going to be shredded if we left them as they were. The wind was now frightening in its intensity.

A few hundred feet to the right of our camp was a col marking the low point between the Central and North Tower of Paine. Beyond it, the North Tower soared steeply upwards, almost as high as the Central Tower. The gap between the two was very small and acted as a wind tunnel, amplifying the gale that was hitting the other side of the towers. As the wind accelerated through the gap it made a deafening roar, like several express trains passing all at once. I took some comfort from knowing that at least we would be descending on the relatively sheltered side of the mountain.

Noel and Paul looked anxious to leave.

'We'd better tie the portaledges down, or there won't be anything left of them when we come back up again,' I shouted into the wind.

I folded my own portaledge up against the rock and secured it with karabiners clipped through each of the top corners into a loop of rope that hung down from the anchors while watching Noel and Paul climb up level with their own. Their position looked precarious, one perched either side of their portaledge, hanging from pieces of rope with one hand, their feet perched unsteadily on small icy ledges. Paul was directing the operation.

'Okay Noel, push it up *now*.'

As they lifted the portaledge and started to fold it into the rock a gust of wind caught it, blowing it back down, knocking them both off balance and leaving them swinging on the ropes. It would have scared me, but neither Noel nor Paul seemed even slightly bothered. I envied their relaxed and comfortable manner in such surroundings. By comparison, I felt very slow and deliberate.

'Right, let's try it again.'

This time the portaledge folded up without difficulty and Paul flattened it against the rock with his body, hastily securing it.

18

I caught Sean's eye while he was busy pushing the last of his belongings into a heavily iced-up rucsac. When I had finished untying from the loop of rope that had acted as my safety line during the night, I shouted across to him.

'I'll get going now. See you on the glacier.'

For a brief moment I wasn't secured to anything and stood on the small ledge feeling very vulnerable before clipping a short sling from my harness on to another rope. I hated these change-overs. With dozens of ropes hanging around the portaledges, it was always difficult to select the right one, and the snow only made things worse. I had visions of clipping into the wrong rope, secured only at one end, slipping, and disappearing into the abyss below. Such accidents are not uncommon. I had once abseiled off the end of a rope in the French Alps. Fortunately it had been on an easy-angled snow slope and, despite over-balancing backwards, I had not fallen. The near miss had shocked me at the time, but I had heard stories of others who were not so lucky. These stories acted as powerful reminders, focussing my thoughts on the simple task in hand.

On this occasion, I had made the right choice. Once I had retrieved it from the snow, I could see that the rope went in an arc from the portaledges to the start of our fixed ropes ten feet to the left. It acted as a safety line between the two. Convinced of my safety, I moved quickly across the ledge to the beckoning rope that ran continuously to the glacier far below.

I admit that while spending so much time and energy fixing it in place I had doubted its usefulness. We were all used to climbing as roped pairs, starting at the bottom of a mountain and going in a continuous push to the summit, or until a retreat seemed necessary, but this technique relies on rapid progress, for it is impossible to carry more than about a week's supply of food and gas. Because we expected the difficult climbing on the Central Tower to take much longer and were worried by the fickle Patagonian weather, we had decided instead to fix a line of ropes up the mountain face. We thought this would allow us to go up and down at will, to resupply, or to escape a storm. It was the usual way of climbing in Patagonia and we hoped it would give us the best chance of success.

Preparing to abseil, I thought only of the warmth, comfort and food in our camp in the forest below. The line of ropes made the camp seem much closer and, for once, I thought the fixed ropes were well worth all the effort fixing them in place.

The rope dropped from ledge to ledge down a short snow slope and into a large corner. Huge updraughts were rising up the corner, swinging me from side to side. I crashed from one wall to the other, my feet peddling ineffectually on the ice-coated rock. In the lulls, spindrift poured down from above, filling the neck of my jacket, only to be blown back up again with the next updraught. After a hundred feet I reached the first belay and had to go through the ritual of changing ropes. The next abseil was steeper. Snow pellets stung my eyes, forcing me to close them almost shut before I leaned out and set off again.

Now I was going quickly, happy to be moving, allowing the rope to slide through my hand. As I cleared a small roof my feet lost contact with the rock and I was hanging free, spinning one way and then the other on the rope. Through blurred vision, I watched the brown of the rock alternate with grey sky. When the spinning stopped and my feet touched the rock again, I continued the steady downward movement.

Pausing at the next change-over, I looked up into the gloom and could just make out figures coming down the ropes above. Beneath me the snow-covered slabs looked none too appealing, and it was impossible to detect the line of ropes buried under the snow that was still pouring down unabated from the face above. Small avalanches were already sliding off steeper parts of the slab. As I approached the first diagonal abseil across the slab I had mixed feelings about being first. If enough snow had already accumulated, I would start an avalanche, but if I crossed safely, the others would be at greater risk as the snow built up further. It was not a problem to dwell on. Even though I was aware of the danger, once I got up a bit of speed I began to enjoy myself. We were retreating, but at least it was orderly, under control, and it would take only a few hours jumaring the ropes to regain our high point.

My joy soon turned to anger as I started to abseil diagonally across the slabs, struggling against the pull of gravity. The first part of the slabs was only thinly covered with fresh snow and my feet slid on the rock underneath. Tensioning on the rope, I managed to get a little traction and moved to the left as well as down, only to slip and pendulum back to the right. I tried again, repeating the process, but this time with a bigger pendulum. Noel was waiting at the belay above.

'Get a move on. I'm freezing up here.'

It was only possible to use each section of rope one at a time. No doubt Paul and Sean were also stuck further up. I stopped trying to control my descent and abseiled straight down until suspended in the bottom curve as the rope arced between two anchors. The rope would go no further through the descender. I cursed myself, the wind, and the snow which still poured down in hardened pellets.

Fired with anger, I grabbed the rope leading to the lower anchor and hauled myself horizontally towards it through thigh-deep snow. After a lot of effort I reached the belay and looked back, at the trench I had created. The image gave me a nervous confidence. If the slope was in imminent danger of avalanche then my actions should have set it off. Quickly I transferred my descender to the next rope.

Suddenly I heard a faint hissing which grew to a loud swooshing sound as the air filled with fresh powder snow. I put my hand over my face as the volume increased, bracing my body as it poured with some force on to my chest and around my ankles. The avalanche didn't last long, but it was enough to send me plunging down the abseil with renewed haste, the change-over to the next rope taking a matter of seconds. Soon my feet were on rock again and I was able to relax a little, having crossed the large snow patch in the centre of the slab. The ropes to the glacier stretched down directly over rock covered in sheets of thin ice.

I peered up into the mist and driving snow. The line of the rope looked unnatural and the others, spaced at regular intervals along it, seemed strangely out of place. Noel was floundering his way across the last of the snow, his face contorted in a grimace of fear and disgust.

The remaining rope lengths to the glacier were relatively straightforward. There was little friction for my feet, so I abseiled with some speed, mostly on my knees or backside. The fun ended at the cone of snow banked up at the bottom of the face. Once again it was back to wading, which soon became more like swimming. I had to struggle hard to make the rope go through the descender, eventually falling on my back as the end finally went through it. For a few moments I floundered in the snow, unable to regain balance without the lifeline I had been tied to for days.

Without the rope I could face outwards and walk down to the base of the snow cone and then out a short distance on to the glacier, where I slumped down to wait for the others. The storm was now worse than any of the previous bad weather. Sitting in the snow, I was mesmerised by the roar of the wind, gusts being forced through the Towers faster than ever. Cloudlets of snow billowed like tornadoes higher up before twisting and turning as they tracked down the glacier past me. It was an awesome demonstration of power. Above the noise I heard a faint shout.

'Ah, Mr Yates. Are you all right?' Noel was ploughing through the snow towards me.

'Yes, I'm fine. I was just listening to the wind.' I felt rather foolish, but Noel just smiled and nodded. He looked eager to leave.

'Do we need to wait for the others?'

'Might as well,' I said. 'We're going to need all the help we can get to wade through this stuff.'

The wait was not long. Paul was soon sliding down with his usual ease, casually bounding down the ropes with big strides and an equally big grin. I wondered if he ever felt fear. Sean was some way behind, employing a more methodical and deliberate style. He looked as safe and reliable as ever. As they came across to join us, Sean looked worried.

'I'm glad that's over. It's – well – dangerous up there.'

As I nodded in agreement, I heard a dull cracking, followed

22

by a roar, coming from above. It sounded like gravel being tipped from a truck. Simultaneously, our faces turned upwards, searching the slabs for the avalanche.

'Look, there it is!'

I followed Noel's pointing finger to an area above and to the left of our line of ropes. A large patch of snow had broken away and was sliding down the icy rock beneath. A surging mass of ice crystals outlined its progress. We stared, motionless, at the overwhelming spectacle. The avalanche poured down the icy slabs towards the bottom of our ropes where a pile of snow was starting to accumulate on the slope immediately above us.

'I think we'd better run for it!' I shouted.

We scattered in all directions, stumbling and falling in the waist-deep snow. When the noise died down, I glanced over my shoulder and saw that the avalanche had stopped. I collapsed in the snow, laughing through gasping breaths. We had been lucky, but our ropes were now buried in a great heap of debris.

I felt angry with myself. It was an unnecessary risk to have taken. Sometimes, when climbing mountains, you have to take risks, usually moving through areas of known danger – places that have to be crossed in order to stand a chance of reaching the summit. It might mean passing beneath an unstable ice-cliff, walking across a gully prone to rock-fall, or climbing a slope that you fear might avalanche. These are always tense moments and all that can be done is to move as quickly as possible in the hope that all will be well. Each individual climber makes his or her own decisions about the level of these objective dangers they are prepared to accept. I was angry because we had not made a calculated decision. We had lingered in bed and spent too long leaving the ledges. During that time enough snow had amassed on the slopes beneath us to make an avalanche probable. We had been forced into a dangerous situation by our own negligence. Fortunately nothing serious had happened except that we had received a bit of a shock and the sickening shallow buzz that comes from a narrow escape.

As we started the walk back across the glacier I heard the rumbling of another avalanche. It started on the large patch of snow we had crossed and cut across the line of our ropes. It was difficult to tell its size, but I felt sure it would have swept any one of us away had we still been abseiling.

The walk across the glacier was shorter than I remembered. We were breaking a fresh trail, and some of the gusts of wind were so strong that it was necessary to stop and let them pass before continuing. Soon we reached a huge buttress of rock that gave some shelter and I knew the worst was over. From here it was all downhill to base camp.

We skipped and slid on our backsides down a short slope to a small saddle where we had stored food and equipment in a snow cave. Earlier in the expedition, before we had reached the ledges and set up the portaledge camp, we had used the snow cave as a shelter. It now had an abandoned look to it. A week earlier it had been the focal point of all our efforts.

I stood staring at the snow cave while the others removed their climbing harnesses. We had dug it into a steep bank of snow, but the entrance had since almost completely drifted over. The bank above had a deep depression where the roof had collapsed. I remembered building it. Sean and I had started digging, but Noel and Paul, who had never built or slept in a snow cave before, had been eager to take over. Before long Sean and I were able to lounge around, eating and making tea, occasionally poking our heads into the hole to offer advice. 'The roof needs to be higher. We need some shelves round the sides. A little longer I think.' It had taken hours until the cave was large enough inside for us to lie down and almost stand up. By the end, Noel and Paul had realised there was no more to making a snow hole than a lot of digging, and they had been left to do most of the work with a lot of laughter at their expense.

'Are you coming, Simon?' Paul had caught me day-dreaming again. The others had already stashed their surplus equipment in the kitbag and were preparing to leave.

'Yeah, I'm on my way.'

I quickly took off my harness, put it in the bag and followed the others down the steep snow slope. At the base of the rock buttress, the going got harder again as we traversed rock slabs covered in snow. I couldn't help feeling depressed. We had been working on the climb for nearly two weeks and our progress had been pitifully slow. We had completed only the easiest part of the route and had reached no more than a third of the way up. Admittedly the weather had been poor and the summer had still to arrive, but it looked as if it could take us another two months to complete the climb. I doubted if I could last that long, mentally or physically. Our chances of success did not look good. If we were to reach the summit, we were going to have to climb a lot quicker on the most difficult part, and the weather would have to improve considerably. Crouching on the rock slab, trying to prevent myself from being blown over while the snow fell relentlessly, neither seemed a remote possibility.

I cheered up when we were able to bum-slide on the fresh snow into a short flat valley that was guarded from the wind coming down the glacier by a ridge of moraine. After days of mind-numbing noise and batterings it was a relief to be in a more sheltered spot. Like a punch-drunk boxer miraculously spared from further blows, I staggered along, rolling from side to side. It was some time before I fully recovered and was able to walk normally.

Taking advantage of the improved conditions, I put on a spurt, leaving the others behind. Base camp was now near, and I relished the thought of rest and some decent food. The days of chocolate, dried soups, mashed potato and tinned fish had satisfied need but left me feeling empty.

At the end of the valley I entered a boulder field. The covering of snow made it difficult to judge where to step or jump, my numbed sense of balance only making matters worse. Falling heavily several times, I cursed the snow and boulders. I was deeply aware of how easy it would be to break an ankle on such ground. After each fall I recomposed myself, willing my tired body and mind. 'Come on, Simon. Don't be stupid. Don't screw up now.' I imagined hypothetical conversations back home.

'How did you break your leg, Simon?'

'Oh, I slipped on a boulder.'

The embarrassment would be unbearable. It was the sort of accident that befalls hapless walkers in the Lake District or Snowdonia.

All too soon it was over, and I was running down a gravel path that followed a small stream, heading for the tree line. I entered the trees, which at this height were more like shrubs, gnarled and twisted from the effects of the wind, their canopy of small waxy leaves horizontal to the ground and only a few inches above it. It looked like a forest of bonsai trees.

As I descended, so the temperature rose and the snow turned to rain. I entered a world of dank, dripping forest, fresh with the earthy smells of early summer. I grabbed handfuls of leaves from low branches, crushing them in my hands to release a beautiful aromatic scent. The forest canopy reduced the wind to little more than a background breeze and I walked slowly, savouring every minute, stopping to examine newly opened flowers and drink from a small stream that flowed down the hillside. It was a far cry from the world of snow, ice and wind above.

The sight of our camp – three wooden huts and a cluster of tents in the forest – flooded me with another wave of relief. On all my previous mountaineering trips base camp had been a group of tents on a bleak, rocky ridge of moraine on the side of a glacier. This place was luxury in comparison.

The largest hut was in better condition than the other two and we had chosen it for our kitchen and living space. It consisted of a simple circle of upright logs, with a roof of thinner branches, covered in layers of polythene sheeting. I slung off my rucsac and stepped inside, remembering our joy when first arriving at the huts after walking up from the valley below, expecting them to be fairly basic. Standing in the doorway, I couldn't help laughing at how wrong we had been. In the far corner of the room was a stone fireplace, its stone and wood chimney painstakingly lined with flattened-out cans. There were shelves on the walls, filled with our food and the table was flanked with two benches. Small inscribed wooden plaques hung above the fireplace, recording the names of previous mountaineering expeditions which had used the hut. It even had a carved wooden telephone hanging on one wall. The place was a living museum, and very comfortable at that. I admired the hundreds of hours of work different climbing groups had put into the place over the years and wished I was as socially minded. But as I listened to the rain falling on the roof, I realised that the surrounding craftwork told another story. Most of it had probably been done through boredom, after sitting out days of storms.

I helped myself to a large piece of cheese, eating it greedily. I had spent days dreaming of such treats and I savoured every mouthful. As I started on a second piece the door opened, startling me and giving me feelings of guilt about my selfish gluttony.

'Hi, Simon.'

Hanneke stood in the doorway. It was nice to see her smiling, pretty face and shoulder length blonde hair after days in the company of three dirty men. I returned her smile self-consciously while cramming down the last chunk of cheese.

'Oh, hi Hanneke. Merry Christmas.'

We had met Hanneke just a few days before leaving Britain. She had heard from a friend of Sean's about our expedition to Patagonia and wanted to join us. We had readily agreed, happy to have one more sharing the considerable costs. Personally, I was glad of her company. It was good to have an outsider to talk to who wasn't completely wrapped up in the climbing.

'How was your trip into town?'

'Fantastic. I've had a great time.'

I felt a pang of envy. 'Well, I'm glad someone's having a good time.'

'How are you getting on up there?'

'We're up to the ledges and we've got the portaledges set up. It's just very slow going.' A feeling of depression swept over me. 'It's awful up there now. We could hardly stand up coming across the glacier. Heaven knows when we'll be able to go back up again.'

Hanneke looked at me sympathetically and quickly changed the subject.

'I bought the food we needed, although I couldn't carry it all. Pepe said he would bring the rest up tomorrow.'

My mood changed as Hanneke started unpacking goodies from her rucsac – fresh bread, chocolate and, most important, Dulce de Leche – a sweet caramel-like spread made from condensed milk. Finally she produced two bottles of pisco, the local spirit which was not unlike Tequila. It looked as if we were going to have a Christmas celebration after all.

The others were arriving and soon we were all gathered in the hut feasting on cheese and Dulce de Leche sandwiches. It was hard to imagine that an hour before we had been battling our way down the fixed ropes and had narrowly avoided being avalanched.

Sean strolled over to the wooden telephone, picked up the receiver and dialled a number.

'Hello, is that Mario's? Can I order five large special pizzas with side salads and garlic bread? We want them delivered to Campamento Torres – and make it quick because we're starving up here!'

I laughed and snatched the bottle of pisco from the table.

'Cocktails anyone?' There was a roar of approval.

I mixed the pisco with orange Tang and some lemon juice in a plastic bucket which we used for washing pots and clothes. To my surprise, the result was more than palatable. We had filled our cups and were standing in the clearing by the huts, toasting each other a Merry Christmas, when a tall, dark-skinned, bearded man ambled into the camp. He was followed by half a dozen middle-aged couples.

'Bonjour!'

The Frenchman looked to be in his mid-thirties, and I asked if he was leading a trekking group, waving the bucket in his face. He produced a mug from his rucsac and accepted the offering. 'Merci. Merci bien.' His group, however, were not as enthusiastic and viewed us from a distance, aloof and suspicious. I tried breaking the ice by approaching them, but the sight of a filthy Englishman with mad staring eyes, waving a bucket, did little to persuade them to join the party. A few did eventually have a small drink, but they soon left for their camp higher up the valley. Paul grinned wryly as they departed.

'D'you think it was something we said?'

I opened another bottle of pisco and the afternoon disappeared in a blur of laughter, eating and drinking. By the early evening I'd had enough and retired to my tent, determined to renew my long-standing love affair with my sleeping bag.

I was surprised when sleep refused to come and my mind raced, reviewing the day's events. It certainly had been a strange one. I wondered how long we would be stuck in the camp and if we were all destined to become carpenters and wood carvers? There were no answers to my questions, but I pondered the possible outcomes anyway. We had stood at the bottom of the Towers two weeks earlier, viewing the face through binoculars, full of optimism. There was a line of weakness on the face and a system of cracks ran all the way up. We had convinced ourselves we could climb it, even though it was much bigger and steeper than anything we had attempted before. Now I wasn't so sure. The weather had been bad, but no worse than we had expected, and with the summer arriving it would be bound to get better. Yet, however I viewed our situation, I kept coming back to our climbing performance. We had been slow and disorganised. If we were gong to have any chance of climbing the mountain, we would have to improve, and quickly.

Eventually my thoughts slowed enough to allow me to fall into a deep sound sleep.

TWO

A Change Of Attitude

I woke feeling refreshed and lay listening to the trees creaking and groaning, swaying in the ever-present wind. Large droplets of water pounded on to the tent from the leaf canopy above. The weather was still bad. Not that it mattered; I was safe, secure and warm. I could relax. There was no rush to do anything.

The small stream between my tent and the huts had swollen to a torrent during the night. Water had leaked through the tent fabric and accumulated in the corners in small puddles. I cursed as I put on my soaking wet clothes. After mopping up the worst of the water and piling my spare clothing on to my sleeping mat, I stepped outside and headed for the toilet.

Crouching in the long grass and cranberry bushes, I stared through the rain. On a good day it was possible to see the Towers. Today all that could be seen was thick grey cloud just above the valley floor. There was snow down to the base of the cloud. So much for summer, I thought.

Things had been different eighteen months ago when we had been travelling and rock-climbing in the south of India. Above a village called Hampi, Paul and I had climbed a huge, rounded granite boulder. It was a magical place. Derelict palaces and temples were set among hills of rocks and banana plantations. As we sat joking on the summit, watching the sun go down over the fantastic landscape, we shared a dream to come and climb in Patagonia. Looking up into the cloud and rain now, I couldn't help thinking the dream had been misguided.

I left the clearing and headed for the kitchen. The crude door of polythene on a wooden frame was already open. I stepped inside, quite unprepared for the sight that greeted me. Noel was trying to start a fire.

'What on earth's happened in here?'

Noel stood up and turned to face me, smiling. 'The hut leaks, I guess. It's got a bit damp, hasn't it.'

'You're not joking.'

The floor was ankle deep in water. On the table unwashed pots and pans were full of filthy water and an open bag of flour was now a horrible paste. The fireplace was flooded. Water was still pouring through the roof. I remembered that Noel was sleeping in one of the other huts.

'And what about your hut?'

Noel laughed. 'Oh, it's about the same. I woke up with water dripping on my head and had to move. I've spent most of the night trying to sleep sitting upright in the only dry corner. My sleeping bag still seems to have got damp though.'

'You'll have to bring a tent next time!'

Noel's indifference to discomfort baffled me. At times I felt convinced that he *wanted* to suffer, that he thought it somehow heightened the experience.

I had met Noel briefly in the Alps some years before. He was a long-standing friend and climbing partner of Paul's, and it was Paul who suggested that Noel should be invited to join us in Chile. I got to know him well while we were planning the expedition. He was tall and thin, but muscular, with an unkempt mop of brown hair. He lived in Oxford and worked on microbiology research at the university. Like many academics, Noel was eccentric, and I often saw a touch of the mad professor in him. He seemed to give little thought to the practicalities of life, but he was friendly and generous, and being with him was great fun. His climbing ability was without question. Having spent the previous summer on the big granite walls of Yosemite in California, Noel had greater knowledge than any of us of the techniques required to climb the Central Tower of Paine.

It was difficult to understand why both Noel and Paul had arrived in Chile without a tent when we were going to spend weeks camping in one of the most inhospitable parts of the world, notorious for its hurricane-force winds and lashing rain. Sean and I were horrified by their lack of concern. When we raised the issue with Paul, he simply dismissed it, confidently saying that it would be all right and that something would turn up. After travelling halfway down Chile on the train, and reaching the end of the line at Puerto Montt, we had unloaded our bags and were searching the carriage to make sure nothing was left behind when Paul pulled something out from under a seat.

'Hey, you'll never guess what I've found!' he said, waving a piece of green folded canvas above his head.

I knew instinctively it was a tent and shook my head, amazed at his luck. It must have been left by one of numerous Chilean back-packers on the train. The tent was small and not in the best condition, but it was better than nothing. Convinced that the tent would not have stood up to the night of rain, I left the hut to check on Paul. He was just getting up and looked surprisingly dry.

'Did you get wet in the night, Paul?' I asked smugly.

'No, I'm perfectly dry.'

I had failed to notice the sheet of polythene strung above his tent. He was not as foolish as I had supposed.

'And what about you, Simes?'

'I got a little damp,' I mumbled uncomfortably. 'Just around the edge of the tent.'

Paul smiled sympathetically as I walked away, cursing life's injustices.

When I first met Paul at the Outdoor Trade's annual show in Harrogate I was impressed by his sense of fun, which was mirrored in his colourful, baggy clothing and the Mohican hairstyle. I had heard and read a lot about his formidable rock-climbing record, his bold routes on the sea cliffs of Anglesey, in the slate quarries around Llanberis and Strone Ulladale on Lewis. They were all serious ascents, and although only twenty-four, Paul already enjoyed cult status among British climbers. I was flattered that he had approached me for advice about an expedition he was planning to India. Looking at his emaciated body, all I could suggest was that he put on some weight. We got on well and spent a lot of time talking and swapping stories. Paul seemed to be a free spirit, an adventurer, living off his wits. When later I heard he had been caught by the police that night, rolling a barrel of beer through the streets of Harrogate, I liked him even more.

By a twist of events, we ended up going to India together. We were both ill and achieved few of our aims, but we had a good time, and the trip cemented our friendship.

I headed back towards the hut, which was now spewing out clouds of white smoke. Inside Noel and Sean were busy discussing breakfast.

'What do you fancy, oatcakes or porridge?'

'It has to be oatcakes. We can put Dulce, peanut butter and jam on them,' said Sean.

'Sounds good. How about some butter as well?'

Their conversation made me laugh. With little to occupy our time in the spells of bad weather, food had taken on an unusual importance. Sean's capacity to tuck away food had earned him the nickname 'Three Plates' from a Pakistani expedition cook, due to the number of helpings he had at each meal. The name and the habit had stuck. We cheered each time Sean went for his third helping of food.

Sean was my regular climbing partner; we had known one another since our university days, although it was a number of years before we started climbing together. His head-down walk and disinterested air disguised a wealth of talents. On the train journey down Chile, there had been a long hold-up during which a crowd had gathered at the front of the train. Sean had gone to investigate, and on his return I had quizzed him about the delay. 'Oh, the train's run over some geezer,' he replied in his casual understated way. When the train moved off again, we passed a man lying dead under a blanket at the side of the track. Although sometimes I got annoyed with his slowness, I deeply admired Sean's skill as a climber, and his judgement. Unlike me, he slowly released his huge reserves of strength and energy, pacing himself so well that I found it impossible to imagine him ever making a serious mistake, or ceasing to plod slowly onwards, regardless of the conditions or his tiredness. Sean's other love was photography. He used the travelling opportunities that came with climbing to amass photographs which he sometimes exhibited back in Britain. When he wasn't climbing, Sean would often disappear for hours at a time with his large metal camera box slung around his neck. I considered him completely reliable and felt safer climbing with him than with anyone else. We had climbed, travelled, worked and lived together for long periods of time and knew each other's strengths and weaknesses. In the extreme situations we often found ourselves, this was reassuring knowledge.

Our breakfast ritual was getting under way, supervised by Noel and Sean. I admired how organised they both were in the kitchen and wondered if we could transfer the efficiency of living in the forest camp to the mountain.

'Do you want the first oatcake, Simon?' Noel passed me a bowl and I eagerly spooned the heavy cake into my mouth.

'Hmm, delicious. Does anyone know what the barometer is doing?'

Paul picked up the small metal instrument hanging on a piece of string by the door.

'The pressure's still low,' he said, throwing it away dismissively.

Noel looked bothered. 'Well I hope this weather doesn't keep up for long. I've got to be back in Oxford in three weeks' time. At the latest.'

'I'm sure it will get better,' I said. 'We're going into summer after all. Mind you, it will take a day or two of decent weather to shift all the snow that's fallen.' As I spoke, I recalled talking to people back in England who had spent weeks in Patagonia and returned home having done no climbing at all.

'We're climbing too slowly. We need to be better organised if we're going to get up this mountain,' Noel said.

The concern, I felt sure, was uppermost in all our minds but it still seemed strange coming from his lips. My efforts to organise things back in Britain had been continually thwarted whenever I tried to involve Noel. He had given me two phone numbers and could never be contacted at either of them. Invariably, just when I had given up the chase, he would call me.

'I agree. We've been pretty bungling up to now,' I added, hoping that a constructive debate would develop.

In truth, it was not only the climbing that was chaotic – our anarchic departure from Britain and progress down South America had been no better. We had hoped to catch a boat from Puerto Montt to the southern tip of Chile. Paul had even spoken to the shipping company by phone from Britain, but when we turned up in their office in the town at the beginning of December, we were told that the boats didn't start running until the middle of January. We had ended up catching a bus, back-tracking several hours of the train journey before crossing the Andes and travelling down the featureless plains of the Argentinian Pampas. It was a weary group that got off the coach three days later, unhappy that the journey had not been by the romantic boat through the Chilean Fiordland as Paul had promised.

'Well, Noel, you've done this sort of climbing before in Yosemite . . .' Sean said.

'It was a picnic compared to his,' Noel interrupted.

'But we're all new to this,' Sean continued. 'We need to know what we are doing wrong and how we can improve it.'

'As I see it, we've got some more work to do fixing rope and hauling bags.'

Paul was nodding in agreement. 'Yeah, remember the trouble we had hauling that bloody bag up the lower slabs, Simes?'

'How could I ever forget it?'

*

It was on our third day of climbing that Paul and I had volunteered to go in front and push out the route while Noel and Sean ferried loads across the glacier and up the rope we had already fixed. It was bitterly cold, with a biting wind blowing round the Towers, carrying in snow showers from the Patagonian ice-cap. The conditions were, to say the least, marginal and it was with great reluctance that we left the comfort of the ice cave and crossed the glacier to start climbing. I reached the top of our ropes, which were marked by two huge canvas sacks, containing our equipment. We had already brought the bags halfway round the world. They had been lugged through airports and bus stations, carried in and out of hotels, packed on horses through Paine's forests and faithfully portered up slopes of moraine and across a glacier to the base of the Tower. It was as if the journey had been some sort of training for pulling them up the mountain. At times I found it hard to decide whether the contents of the bags would enable us to reach the top or prevent it.

I tied into the ropes and prepared to lead the first pitch of the day. The climbing had been relatively straightforward up to our high point, our progress aided by ropes left from a previous Spanish attempt. Paul soon joined me and prepared the belay. Above us the ropes disappeared into deep snow.

Once everything was sorted, I stepped off the small platform accommodating Paul and the bags and on to the snow-covered slab. The climbing was immediately precarious. My feet sank knee-deep in the powdery snow and my crampons skidded ineffectually on the rock beneath. The only way to make progress was to compact the snow gently with each foot and then carefully transfer all my weight up on to it. Soon the snow became shallower and my feet slipped at each step, gripping only when my crampons caught on features in the rock. It was impossible to know what I was standing on, and I imagined that my crampons were simply resting on quartz crystals. At any moment they could crumble, catapulting me down the slab. I managed to excavate a horizontal crack, which for a brief time provided a handrail and enabled me to keep my balance, but it was not long before the slab became bare rock devoid of footholds. An idea came in a flash. I pushed the shaft of an ice axe into the crack and pulled down on its head. It seemed to hold my weight. Rigging some nylon slings to it, I was able to put a foot into them and transfer my whole weight on to it. Much to my surprise, the axe held, allowing me to traverse the crack by leap-frogging from one axe to another, and so reach some deeper snow again.

I teetered up the rest of the pitch without incident, though not without anxious moments. It had taken hours, but at least I'd been warm. Paul looked frozen. He freed one of the sacks, tied it to one of my ropes and started climbing the other rope while I hauled up the sack. Slowly it rose diagonally, ploughing a trench in the snow as it went. It took all my strength and weight on the rope to haul it just inches at a time. It was only when the sack came out of the deep snow and on to the bare rock slab that I saw our mistake. The sack slid sideways, and while we watched helplessly, it picked up speed and went bouncing across the slope in a huge arc, eventually stopping under an overlap. I tried pulling it up, but it was wedged tight.

'Paul. The bloody sack's stuck. You'll have to go down and free it,' I shouted.

'Okay, I'm on my way,' came the reluctant reply.

With a lot of difficulty he was able to abseil down the rope he had been coming up and swing across to hang below the sack.

'Right, Simes – pull!'

I pulled with all my might as Paul pushed, but still the sack would not budge.

'It's no good. You'll have to try something else,' I yelled down.

Several more joint efforts produced no better results. I slumped on the belay, exhausted, while Paul wriggled in the snow next to the sack. It was only when he got under the sack and levered it into a piggy-back position that I realised what he was doing. I gave the rope a hard tug and the sack bounced up across the overlap. With Paul climbing up his rope next to the sack and pushing it upwards as I pulled, we managed to get it up to the belay. Paul hung, panting, on the belay beside me.

'We can do without this!' he said.

We had moved ourselves and the sack a mere hundred and fifty feet. It had taken half the day.

'Well, it's your lead now. Any bright ideas for bringing the sack up the next pitch?'

Paul shrugged his shoulders as he prepared to leave the belay. 'If you clip it to you, that might stop it swinging sideways.'

Anxious to make up the lost time, Paul flailed up through the deep snow above the belay with great speed. I sat watching, paying out the rope, interested in how he would cope with the ice and snow. Paul was a rock-climber and had only recently started climbing snow and ice. His experience was limited to walking over a few glaciers in the Alps and a week spent ice-climbing in Scotland the previous winter.

There was a certain unfamiliarity in his motion which made him look slightly out of control, but I never thought for one moment he was going to fall. Towards the end of the pitch the deeper snow once again ran out. Paul stepped delicately off it and into a thin runnel of ice and balanced up it. His axes and crampons were only just biting – a fall would have had serious consequences. Like the sack, he would whip in an arc and smash into the rocky overlaps far below. I held my breath as he inched towards a piece of old rope sticking out from the ice above. Almost in one movement his feet slipped, suspending him from just the points of his axes. He calmly regained his balance, skipped his feet up the ice, locked his left arm and reached up to grab the piece of rope. His feet skidded again, but the difficulty was over; his other hand was already on the rope. Within seconds he was monkeying up it. Now it was my turn.

Climbing the diagonal rope was trouble enough, but with the sack clipped to me it was exhausting. Paul pulled the sack from above at all the right times, but it seemed to have a mind of its own. With every step it lurched behind me and fell in a small pendulum, pulling me off my feet. Each time I cursed, regained my balance and then repeated the process over again. Eventually I arrived at the belay and collapsed in the snow.

'We're still not doing this right, are we?' I moaned.

Paul was already studying the ground ahead. 'It should be easier when we start hauling it straight up.'

'I suppose you're right,' I said wearily. 'But I'm stuffed already.' I put my arm affectionately round the sack. 'What say we get this beast to the bottom of that steep wall over there and call it a day?'

'Yeah, okay.' Paul nodded as he spoke.

It was just a short distance over easy-angled snow to where the old Spanish ropes reappeared once more beneath the wall. I raced up to the ropes and Paul quickly followed, dragging the sack behind. We stood silently for a few minutes, looking up the ropes which soared over an overhang and into a steep corner. Then, fixing my descender on to the rope, I took a look at the sack hanging from the belay. It had taken most of the day to move it up three hundred feet.

'Let's clear off,' I said, giving the sack a swift kick, before sliding off down the rope.

*

We all stared at Noel intently, waiting for his words of wisdom. The situation seemed ironic. Three semi-nomadic, non-conformist climbers, waiting for advice from a non-conformist, perpetual academic. Our only common uniting bond, if there was one, appeared to be avoiding society's hierarchy and responsibilities. Yet here we were mimicking it, taking on fixed roles, eagerly waiting to be organised by the man who had turned up without a tent.

'If the leader takes up the fixing line and secures it at the next belay, it will be easier for whoever goes second to climb that, rather than climbing one of the lead ropes, which is what we have been doing up to now.'

Noel's comment made sense. All the lead climbing had been done on ropes that stretched to absorb the energy that would be created in the event of a fall. This quality allows a fall to be arrested safely, without the rope breaking or putting a great shock on the belay or climber. However, once each pitch had been led safely we had been fixing in place cheaper rope that did not stretch, as it would not have to hold a fall. Besides, without the stretching, it was easier to climb up.

'If there is enough spare fixing rope, let's use that for hauling the kitbag,' Noel continued. 'And if the leader hauls while the second one is climbing, they should be able to free the bag if it gets stuck.'

The advice was beginning to sound familiar. Paul and I had spent a whole day learning what Noel had just told us. I wondered why we had waited so long to discuss it. Perhaps our enthusiasm had got the better of us. When we had arrived at the camp, the weather had been good, and consequently we had rushed up to the bottom of the Towers and started climbing. There had been little time to take stock and get organised.

'What about the hauling itself. Can we do that better?' I asked.

'I'll show you how I do it.'

Noel stepped outside the hut and returned with a selection of climbing equipment which he used to demonstrate a system for hauling.

Paul looked at the pulley before saying, 'Well, I think we're doing that right. Is there anything else we need to know?'

'No, that's the end of my sermon for today. Any chance of another oatcake, Sean?'

'Coming right up.'

I watched Noel visually track the cake's progress from pan to bowl and across the hut. As always, he ate as if he had just come off a hunger strike. His feeding seemed like our efforts so far. There was certainly no lack of individual enthusiasm; indeed that seemed to be part of our problem. We had not been working as a team. In our rush to get on with the climbing we had acted individually and failed to pool our experience. It was only now, forced into inactivity by the storm, that we had stopped to think and plan – something which we should have done before even starting to climb.

It had all seemed so simple back in England. Paul and I had found two friends, both very capable climbers who shared our dream of climbing a new route on the Central Tower of Paine. Together, in Wales and in the Peak District, we had climbed, eaten, drunk, laughed and made plans. Noel and Paul would deal with steep technical rock-climbing while Sean and I would lead on the snow and ice and help the others to cope with the unfamiliar mountain environment. Between us we could climb the steepest rock, the hardest black ice, or any other difficulties we were likely to encounter. In the cosy surroundings of Sheffield front rooms and Oxford pubs, it had seemed the perfect combination. We would laugh ourselves to the summit of the Central Tower. Now, two weeks into the climbing, already our illusions were shattered. We were well and truly stalled.

'I've been thinking,' I said. 'It's obvious that if we want to climb this thing, we might have to do it in bad weather. We certainly have to make the most of any good weather . . .'

'Now the portaledges are in place,' Paul interrupted, 'we can sleep on the face and work from them. That should save us a lot of time going up to our high point each day.'

'Yeah, you're right,' I continued. 'It'll work better if we split into pairs and climb in shifts of two or three days at a time.'

'Hey, Paul,' Noel said enthusiastically, 'do you fancy taking the first shift. That overhanging scoop above our high point looks ace. It would be great to climb that.'

'Yeah, I'm on, Noel. Let's get back up there as soon as the weather clears.'

Sean was still stooped over the fire. He seemed to have perfected a technique for eating oatcakes without disrupting their preparation. He looked engrossed.

'What do you think, Sean?' I wondered if he had been listening.

'Sounds sensible to me. For the time being. We might need to move the portaledges higher once rope is fixed a good way above them, but we can deal with that when we come to it. Anyone want another oatcake?'

Breakfast went on for most of the morning and was only interrupted to stop up some of the leaks in the hut roof and collect more firewood. It finally finished when the enormous bowl of oatcake mixture was exhausted. I left the hut as Sean and Noel began discussing what to have for lunch.

I wandered away from the camp and into the forest. It was good to escape the intense atmosphere of the camp and spend some time alone. The rain had eased during the morning, but the mountains were still shrouded in thick cloud. The snowline was lower. Wind continued to rush over the forest canopy in waves, but it no longer troubled me. I was too absorbed in the beauty of the place, the elegant trees and the radiant, pale green undergrowth. In the rocks by small streams clumps of delicate red flowers were starting to bloom. It was a far cry from the drab December days we had left behind in England. I felt grateful, lucky to have the freedom and opportunity to climb and travel, to see and spend time in such a place.

I followed one of the small streams downhill towards the river and entered a clearing littered with up-ended trees, their twisted bleached limbs all lying in the same direction, as if brushed into place by some huge broom. My stomach churned at the thought of the gust of wind that had flattened such a large area of forest.

The river itself was in spate and its foaming water was cloudy and grey with glacial dust. Something caught my eye upstream and a bird surfaced from the water. It hopped on to a rock just a few feet away and stood preening itself, not in the least bothered by my presence. The bird was striking, a chestnut brown head and breast, with black and white striped back and wings. In appearance, it looked like a cross between a duck and a cormorant. I had seen nothing like it before.

The bird dived back into the water, surfacing some time later a little upstream. The little creature fascinated me, and for a while I stood on the riverbank in the wind and gentle rain watching it, oblivious to all else, before making my way slowly back to the hut.

Inside, Noel was stooped over a pan in the fire. It smelt like curry.

'Hey, Noel, I've just seen a beautiful bird, swimming in the river.'

'That'll be a Torrent Duck. They're only found in Patagonia and are quite rare.'

'Need any help with lunch?' To my surprise, Noel quickly warmed to my offer. Being so interested in food, he and Sean had done most of the cooking and they didn't usually invite assistance from others.

'Well, I've got the food covered, but . . .' – he smiled as he pointed to the pile of filthy cups, plates and pans on the table – '. . . the pots need washing.'

Silently cursing myself for failing to spot the trap, I reluctantly took the pots outside to the small trough. It looked as if it had been abandoned by gold prospectors, crudely made as it was from pieces of tree trunk and fed by a hollowed out branch from the stream. Unfortunately it was perfect for washing up. I'd only just begun on the pots when someone slapped me on the back. I jumped up, startled, and turned round to face the familiar bearded grinning face.

'Hi, man. How's it going?'

Pepe had obviously learned his English from Hollywood movies as well as American tourists. Or else he had lived in the United States for some time; perhaps he even had relatives there. He was softly spoken and gentle, despite his fierce appearance, with matted shoulder-length brown hair and spiky beard.

'Oh hello, you gave me a fright. We're all okay, but we could do with some better weather.'

Pepe nodded sympathetically. 'I've brought the rest of your food – and a few extras.' He produced a carton of wine from his rucsac.

'Come on in. You're just in time for lunch.'

Pepe's services had been recommended to us by people who had visited the area before. He had met us at the roadhead and packed all our food and kit up to the camp on his horses. Pepe lived a simple life, spending the summer months in a tiny hut he had built near to the Estancia Paine, making a modest living hiring out packhorses to visiting trekkers and climbers. Although only in his mid-thirties, he had given up his job as a boat designer in Punta Arenas for a wilderness life, returning to the town for only the winter months. We had all warmed to his generosity and relaxed friendly manner.

The others appeared from their tents, roused by the sound of Pepe's voice. It was not long before the wine was flowing freely.

'Ah don't geddit,' Pepe said. 'Why you guys back down here? How you getting on?'

'Well, it's been sort of slow going,' said Paul. 'But we're up to the ledges and the bags left behind by the Spanish team.'

Pepe's eyes lit up at the mention of the bags. 'How much equipment is up there?'

'Nine bags in all. They've left all sorts of crap up there.' Paul's voice rose an octave as he spoke. 'Loads of rope, climbing gear, clothes, stoves, food – and portaledges. Everything that's needed to climb the wall about twice over. It must have taken ages to get it all up there. Water has got into most of the bags though. Nearly all the kit is ruined. We did get these though.' With a broad smile he shook the front of the large blue and orange down duvet he was wearing. Noel was wearing an identical jacket.

'Are there any ice axes up there?' Pepe asked.

'If we find any axes, we'll bring you one down,' I said.

It was Pepe who had told us of the previous attempts by the Spanish Gallego brothers to climb the Central Tower's East Face. They had already made two visits and spent months on the face. It was rumoured that they would return shortly to complete the climb. Pepe did not like them, and they had made few friends in the area. The wardens in the small hut where we had registered on entering the Parque Nationale Torres Del Paine had even asked us to remove the unsightly bags from the mountain. The mess had incensed us all.

*

44

I remembered standing on the strip of glacial moraine beneath the Towers for the first time. None of us had seriously thought we were about to climb such a daunting monolith of rock. The dreams and plans back in Britain had done little to prepare us for the sight before our eyes. The reality was sobering, but at the same time exhilarating. Nervously, we had taken it in turns to examine the face through binoculars belonging to Noel's mother. Slowly, we had started picking out features, the lines of the routes already climbed and the possibilities for new routes between them. We looked for good lines linked by systems of cracks, corners and chimneys in the rock – features we knew we would have a good chance of climbing. It had not taken us long to spot the cluster of bags left by the Spaniards, hanging about a quarter of the way up the best looking unclimbed line. It was the cleanness of the line that drew us to the climb they had already started.

Their ropes proved to be less help than we had expected, buried as they were beneath snow and ice left over from the winter. It was only after the low-angled slabs were climbed that they were fully exposed. We shamelessly used their ropes to make rapid progress up the last three hundred feet of steep ground to reach the Spanish high point, arriving late in the day. There was little time to celebrate or to examine the abandoned bags. By the time we had fixed our own ropes and descended to the glacier, it was nearly dark.

The following morning we reclimbed our ropes with rucsacs laden with kit needed to transfer camp from the glacier to the wall itself. For the first time the wind had dropped and there was only a slight breeze. We were able to sit on the ledges, bathing in the early morning sun and savour our situation. The modest gain in height of the previous day had taken us above the lower mountains to the east, opening up a new, more extensive panorama, with its rolling hills and turquoise lakes of the park to the south and on the far horizon the flat Pampas. The view was quite unlike any mountain panorama I'd seen before. There were no other high peaks; the Towers reared up from a few tiny foothills.

We eagerly dug the Spanish bags from the snow and opened them up. Most of them contained useless rusting climbing gear and frozen ropes, while Sean found a bag full of ancient portaledges. Noel and Paul had the best luck with first a bag of food and stoves and then, as Sean and I watched enviously, they emptied a bag of clothing, proudly displaying the two duvets. I remembered the pair of them at the start of one of the many snow storms, laughing and joking as they put on old tattered cagoules donated to them by Noel's caring mother. It was obvious that the jackets were totally inadequate for the conditions, and only after finding the duvets did they have sufficient protective clothing.

The discovery set me wondering. As experienced mountaineers, Sean and I were supposed to be passing on our hard-gained wisdom to Noel and Paul – how to climb ice and snow, how to cope with the cold and dampness of mountain living, how to find shelter and react to the ever-changing conditions. In reality, there was little we could teach them about climbing as they were both so talented that they would be able to adapt themselves to almost any technical difficulties. But it remained our job to show them how to look after themselves in such a hostile place. So far Noel and Paul had either ignored or forgotten all our advice on clothing or equipment. Perhaps it had not seemed important, or they reckoned that their confidence and drive would see them through. Clearly Sean and I had been inadequate teachers. We rarely insisted, and simply expected good ideas to be noticed and copied. Fortunately it had turned out well for Noel and Paul; first a tent and now some duvets had been found, but I couldn't help wondering how much longer their luck would hold. They could find themselves in serious trouble if they didn't pay a bit more attention to basic essentials.

The following day we reclimbed the ropes with the last of the equipment for the portaledge camp. It was to be our first night sleeping out on the face. The near perfect weather of the previous day had gone and black threatening clouds were blowing in from the Patagonian ice-cap. It was cold, and we hurried up the ropes, hoping to reach the safety and shelter of the portaledge camp before the inevitable storm. We were about half way up our ropes when the snow started, forcing us to stop and put on more clothing. I joined the others huddled on a belay near the end of the snow-covered slabs. Sean looked most uncomfortable.

'My hands are freezing. I just can't seem to get them warm today,' he said.

I noticed he was wearing only a thin pair of inner gloves. I had on a pair of thick mittens over my inner gloves and both Noel and Paul had been using their mittens since the start of the day. I stared at Sean, puzzled.

'Why don't you put your overmitts on?'

Sean tried to avoid my gaze. 'I left them up on the ledges yesterday,' he muttered.

'Well, I haven't got a spare pair,' I said, looking at Noel and Paul. 'Have either of you got a spare pair of gloves?' They both shook their heads. 'It looks like you're going to get cold hands then,' I said bluntly, amazed at Sean's oversight. 'I think we'd better get going again. The sooner Sean is reunited with his gloves the better.' I clipped into the next section of rope and prepared to leave. Noel was busy taking off his mittens.

'D'you want to use mine, Sean?'

'Yeah, that would be great, Noel.'

I stared at the pair of them in disbelief. I felt enraged.

'And what are you going to use for mittens, Noel?'

'Oh, I'll be all right without any,' he replied with a shrug.

Noel obviously didn't see the injustice and was prepared to sacrifice his own hands for Sean's mistake. He handed the mittens over to Sean, who seemed oblivious to my anger.

'Great, Noel. Thanks a lot.'

'You must be crazy,' I snapped. 'Don't give them to him! If you had a spare pair, sure, but not your *only* pair.'

'I'll be fine, Simon. Don't worry.'

'Well don't complain to me if you get frostbite,' I hissed, starting to climb the next rope.

Later, Noel arrived at the portaledge camp complaining of

cold hands and spent a long time trying to warm them. Fortunately his generosity caused nothing more than a bad session of hot aches.

Our first night on the portaledges was very comfortable. Using the hanging stoves salvaged from the Spanish kit bags, it was possible to cook the following morning without getting up. I thought of all the cramped bivouacs I had spent sitting on tiny ledges, my feet dangling in space, cocooned in a web of rope to prevent a fall. The portaledges were luxury in comparison, making me wonder why I'd never used them before.

The shattered pillar of rock above and to the right of the camp was the next feature to climb. It led up to a continuous system of cracks, which we hoped would take us all the way to broken ground near the summit of the Central Tower. Paul and Noel thought it would give them the perfect opportunity to practise their rock-climbing skills while Sean and I could have an easy day sorting out the camp.

From the portaledges we had a perfect view of the day's climbing without even leaving the comfort of our sleeping bags. Through the swirling mist and snow I watched Paul's figure balancing up the rock. Each laboured move came between long pauses spent blowing alternately into each bare hand. The climbing was too difficult to manage while wearing gloves. Eventually, after hours of effort, Paul disappeared round the far side of the pillar, Noel followed him. At the end of the day they slid down their ropes and into our view.

When they arrived at the portaledges, they both looked drained and cold, and Paul quickly put on his duvet. I handed them warm drinks, which they gulped down eagerly. Noel then decided to climb up to their portaledge and get into his sleeping bag, but Paul went on standing next to me, waiting for the food Sean and I were preparing. As time went on his face became pale, his lips blue and he started shaking uncontrollably.

'Why don't you get into your sleeping bag?' I asked, beginning to feel concerned. 'We can pass your food up to you.' Paul's gaze looked distant and for a moment I thought he hadn't heard me.

'I'm fine here, thanks.'

He looked far from all right to me, and it was becoming colder by the minute. What worried me most was Paul's distant look, as if he were in some sort of trance. I had seen that look before.

I remembered my friend Tommy Curtis, sitting in the snow on the summit of a mountain in Pakistan, after a particularly long and tiring day's climbing, while the rest of us took it in turns to dig a snow hole in which to spend the night. Tommy was too tired to help. When the hole was finished, the others crawled inside. Tommy continued to sit outside, staring into space, even though it was now bitterly cold. When I asked him if he was going to get into the snow cave, he said that he was so wet from the previous night that he didn't think it was worth it; he would just sit on his rucsac and wait for the morning to come. I tried to persuade him that it would be much warmer in with the others, but he would have none of it. Eventually, I told him bluntly to get inside. He was too cold and weak to argue and slowly crawled into the entrance, where the others helped him into his sleeping bag. His blank careless expression remained etched in my mind.

I watched Paul for a few more minutes. He too looked as if he no longer cared. Just when he needed his mind to be sharp to deal with his exhaustion and the cold, it appeared to have disengaged, as if some subconscious decision had been made to prevent any further suffering. Such a decision could only make matters worse. Eventually I could take no more.

'Paul, I really think you should get into your sleeping bag.'

My comment seemed to pass Paul by, without the slightest flicker of recognition. I suddenly snapped and started shouting.

'Paul! For Christ's sake, get into your sleeping bag!'

He shook his head and focussed his now alert eyes on mine. They were full of sadness and hurt. My remark had come from nowhere, an act of frustration at not getting my own way, and instantly I regretted being so harsh.

Paul said nothing, but stood silently for a short time longer, before moving sideways to the section of rope leading up to the double portaledge. He climbed the rope to join Noel above, leaving me staring out into space, wondering how much I had hurt him.

*

Pepe looked around the hut uneasily. The wine was finished and the day was getting on.

'Well, guys, I guess I'd better go back. I gotta take a group of trekkers up to the Glacier Grey tomorrow. If you get bored up here, come down and pay me a visit.' Pepe got up to leave. With his typical politeness, Noel rose with him.

'Thanks for the offer, but we want to get back on the mountain as soon as the weather clears.'

Pepe gave Noel a knowing look and smiled.

'I might see you all in a few days' time then. Last year it rained all summer.'

In one swift movement he was out of the door, echoing our chorus of goodbyes. We sat looking gloomily at each other, listening to the sound of water dripping on the hut roof. The silence was finally broken by Sean sifting through food packets. Paul leaned over and whispered in my ear.

'Three Plates is hungry again.'

I looked at Noel and pointed towards Sean. We all sat, hands over mouths, trying to contain our laughter. Eventually Sean raised his head and turned to look at us.

'What do you fancy for dinner?'

THREE

⚒

Back
to the
Fray

I stood outside my tent in the darkness of the Patagonian night, my head torch creating a thin beam of light, picking out tree trunks and droplets of water on their leaves. The camp was dark and silent. I had little idea of the time, or when the conversation and laughter of the others had died down. Bored with the idle chatter, I had retired to my tent early and became absorbed in a book.

Our small collection of books was already circulating. I had been reading Noel's book on Chile. The passage about Patagonia and its tragic history was particularly interesting. As in other parts of the New World, white settlers had dispossessed the native people. As a result, over a short period of time many had died from starvation or epidemics of disease. Those that remained were slaughtered, often invited by settlers to parties where they got the aboriginals drunk and shot them. Their methods had obviously been very effective. All that remains of the four tribes that inhabited Patagonia a hundred and fifty years ago are a few dozen people in the South of Tierra del Fuego. The book both captivated and saddened me. It was only the need to go for a pee that stopped me reading and took me into the forest.

Outside, something seemed strangely different, somehow changed. I stood for a while trying to figure out what it was. Then it struck me – the wind had dropped. I had become so used to a hurricane force gale blasting through the forest canopy that my mine had become numbed to it. It had become simply background noise. Now, at last, it had stopped.

I turned my head torch off and peered up through the trees. It took a while for my eyes to adjust, but gradually they focussed on a few stars. Out above the boulder field at the side of the camp, the Milky Way formed a thick white band arcing across the sky, disappearing behind the dark silhouettes of the Towers. I rotated my head, trying to take in the enormity of the southern sky. I couldn't remember seeing so many stars from summits in the Himalayas. Not even on the best day had the tops of the Towers remained clear. There was not the slightest breath of wind. I wanted to rush back into the camp and wake the others, imagining they would not believe me should another storm blow in. I desperately hoped the weather would hold.

In the morning there was birdsong, and bright light dappled with the shadows of leaves filtered into the tent. I quickly unzipped the tent door, just to confirm what I already knew. The weather was still fine. The others were already up and busy. Clothes hung from makeshift lines strung between trees and smoke poured from the hut chimney. For the first time in days there was a reason for getting up rather than lingering in the tent. I wasted no time in getting dressed.

Over at the hut, Noel and Paul were sorting through piles of soggy clothing and equipment which had been stored in the small lean-to by the door. It was good to see a sense of purpose returning to the camp after the days of forced inactivity. With the reading matter dwindling, I had been secretly dreading the day when all forms of bad weather entertainment were exhausted and, like so many of the hut's previous occupants, we would be reduced to whittling wooden sculptures. The reappearance of the sun mercifully saved us from such mind-numbing activities, if only for the time being. Still, despite the boredom we all suffered waiting in the camp during bad weather, at least the place was safe. I had spent time in other camps where that was not the case.

When Sean and I had arrived in Pakistan a year earlier on the Anglo-Polish expedition to attempt a first winter ascent of Nanga Parbat – the world's ninth highest mountain – we had installed our base camp at a small grassy meadow in an ablation valley at the side of the Rupal Glacier. It seemed an ideal spot; there was a good supply of spring-water nearby which we were told would not freeze up, we could pitch our tents on the flat grass rather than the usual glacial ice and we were a good safe distance from the enormous 15,000-foot Rupal Face of the mountain, which reared up from the head of the glacier.

At first, all went well. We settled into the camp and started climbing, making good initial progress on the massive face in a spell of fine settled weather. Then the weather turned, forcing us down and confining us to camp. For day after day we suffered continual snowfall and plummeting temperatures, making life a misery. It became necessary to wear full down suits, just to stay warm in the camp during the day. The climbing was put on hold.

Eventually, after a particularly windy night, one morning brought a return to stillness and clear skies. The storm had finally blown itself out. We all emerged from our tents and stood in the dazzling light reflected from the deep fresh snow, staring up at Nanga Parbat which looked particularly beautiful in its brilliant white coating. High up, it was still windy and huge plumes of snow streaked across the sky from the summit ridges. As we watched, avalanches poured down the mountain-side above.

The following day, four of the Poles decided to return to the mountain and make their way up to camp one. Much of the snow had cleared, but many slopes were still in a dangerous condition, with a high risk of avalanche. But there would always be some avalanche risk in the Himalayas in winter, they reasoned, and we needed to take advantage of this spell of good weather.

'There go the avalanche triggers,' I announced jokingly

when the Poles left camp, hiding my anxiety that they would not be caught in one.

Watching them wade across the glacier and then plough up a hillside of chest-deep snow before disappearing from sight did little to improve my confidence. It was a relief when they radioed to say they had reached camp one.

That night I slept well, knowing the Poles were safe as camp one was situated on a ridge out of any avalanche danger, only to wake suddenly the next morning to a deafening crashing sound. The crash turned to a roar and then a rumble coming from up the valley. I had just started to relax again when the blast hit my tent, flattening it instantly and pinning the fabric to my face. I started struggling to breathe and pushed my arms against the terrific force pressing from outside, trying to maintain a space. It was a battle just to keep a few inches in front of my face. I knew that the camp had been hit by an avalanche and reasoned that at any moment I would be buried in thousands of tons of debris, if it wasn't happening already. This is it, I thought; you're going to be killed by an avalanche in base camp. It didn't seem fair.

Then it stopped and there was silence. I tried to free myself, but the weight of snow above me prevented it. I heard muffled voices and knew I could not be deeply buried. As I thrashed around once more someone approached my tent.

'Are you all right, Simon?' I barely recognised Jon Tinker's voice.

'Yeah, get me out of here!' I shouted back.

A few minutes later Jon returned with a shovel and dug me out. I stood silently with the others in the devastation that just a few minutes before had been our base camp. It was ruined.

Quickly we pieced together what had happened. About 10,000 feet up the Rupal Face was a scar where a huge serac had broken off. The thousands of tons of ice had then fallen the length of the face to the glacier below. Although we were more than three miles from that point, the blast and airborne debris had carried on down the glacier to our base camp.

The force with which the blast had hit the camp was evident all around. All the tents were completely flattened. The large metal-framed mess tent was squashed, its poles buckled and canopy shredded. Plastic barrels containing equipment and food, weighing forty to fifty pounds each were four hundred yards down the valley, along with most of our personal kit which had been sucked from the tents. But no one was hurt. We had been lucky.

Later, after the initial shock had subsided, we were able to laugh at the event, and especially at the expedition doctor Christophe, who in his panic to escape the avalanche had ripped both his sleeping bag and tent in half. Ironically the avalanche triggers up at camp one had not been affected.

We set about repairing the damage to the camp but were never able to feel comfortable in it again. Every small rumble coming from the direction of the Rupal Face had to be checked.

*

Noel greeted me with his usual childlike enthusiasm, which had been noticeably absent over the previous few days.

'Morning, Simon. We're going up again later today. That's if the weather holds, of course.'

'Oh, I think it will,' I said. 'I got up in the middle of the night and it was perfectly still and clear. I've a feeling we're in for a good spell.'

'I can't wait to get back up there again, Paul.' Noel was gesticulating wildly as he spoke, mimicking strange contorted climbing movements. 'It's going to be brilliant. Cranking our way up that perfect granite.'

I remembered the tortuous coach journey through the Argentinian Pampas. In the monotonous flat landscape there had been the occasional escarpments, some displaying small cliffs, and Noel and Paul had become highly excited with each outcrop of rock, pointing out potential climbs to one another. At times they had got so worked up that I seriously wondered if they were going to stop the coach to satisfy their seemingly insatiable desire to climb. In Puerto Montt, only two days into our journey, they had even climbed a radio mast as nothing else was available.

Although I warmed to their enthusiasm, I felt excluded. Only as a teenager, newly introduced to climbing, had I experienced it with such intensity. Sean also seemed to have a more reserved attitude. Perhaps our years of mountaineering, with all its associated waiting and disappointment, had mellowed us, or turned us into cynics.

'Where's Sean?' I asked, interrupting their private debate.

'In the kitchen,' Paul replied with a nod of his head in that direction.

'I should have guessed.'

Sean was busy making porridge, the alternative breakfast to oatcakes.

'The kettle's just boiled, if you want a brew,' he said.

I helped myself to a cup of coffee and slumped down by the table.

'Do you reckon the fresh snow will have cleared?' I said with a note of concern in my voice. The sun would heat up the snow-laden slopes and strip them down to the hard base. There would be avalanches, and we'd already had one narrow escape.

'Most of it should have gone by evening, if the weather stays fine,' Sean said, 'And it won't affect the climbing above the ledges where it's steep.'

'Yeah, I guess you're right. I'm just worried about the slabs at the bottom.'

'Oh, I think they'll be all right. We're certainly not going to get up the mountain by sitting down here in the forest.'

Sean was right. If we were to have any chance of reaching the top, we would have to get back on the mountain as quickly as possible and take every opportunity to climb .

We spent the day drying clothes and lazing in the sun. By early evening we were all sitting in the hut for a final meal together. All was ready. Paul's and Noel's rucsacs were carefully packed with clothing, sleeping bags and enough food for three days, the length of time they hoped to spend on the face. Then, as we had agreed, Sean and I would climb up to the portaledges and take over from them.

There was a pensive atmosphere in the hut during the meal.

No one spoke about anything more than the meal. I sensed that the climbing and our approach to it was taking on a more serious note. We had reached a turning point. The time had come to capitalise on our efforts, and I felt a little sad. When we had all been together on the mountain, a sense of fun had prevailed. The responsibilities of decision making, route finding, climbing and sack hauling had been shared. Someone could always be relied upon to be the joker. Now we would be climbing in isolated pairs. There would be more work, responsibility, worry and danger. If anything went seriously wrong, or somebody was injured, it would be up to each pair to deal with it.

Eventually Paul rose to his feet and smiled at Noel.

'I guess we should go.'

Noel looked hesitant. 'Another brew perhaps?'

'No,' said Paul, shaking his head. 'We want to reach the portaledges before it gets dark.'

He walked outside. Noel gulped down his drink and followed him. I felt the tension that had built during the meal ebb away.

'See you in three days,' Paul said before turning and setting off towards the Towers with Noel at his heels.

'Yeah, give it your best, guys,' Sean said encouragingly.

'Take care,' I added feebly, but they were already gone and I doubt if they heard me.

*

Three days later Sean and I were once more slogging our way up the steep, winding path towards the Torres Glacier. For once the sun shone on our backs. The Towers looked incongruous set against the almost clear summer sky, like superimposed images in a science fiction 'B' movie. A small cap of cloud hung over the summit of the Central Tower. To the east, big lenticular clouds, shaped like flying saucers, hovered motionless above the Pampas. It was a perfect New Year's Day.

I felt glad to be moving after a week of inactivity, realising with gained height and an ever broadening horizon how claustrophobic the camp in the forest had become. It had been quiet and dull while Noel and Paul were away on the mountain. Sean and I got on, but we had little new or interesting to say. After years of climbing together and sharing houses in Sheffield, we knew one another too well.

I paused at the base of the short gully leading up to the top of the moraine ridge. The Towers were now close and from the ridge I would be able to see them fully. Up above the Central Tower a pair of condors were soaring effortlessly, spiralling up and down in tight circles, riding the turbulent air. I watched them for a while before putting my head down and setting off quickly up the gully, anxious to see the others. The slope of delicately balanced chunks of shale, proved as awkward as ever, our steps often having to be repeated as the shale collapsed beneath them. Towards the top my patience snapped and I made a dash for the ridge. I must have looked a comic sight, snatching at rocks which invariably came away in my hands, pedalling wildly with my feet as rocks cascaded down the slope below. Once on the ridge, I collapsed among a group of large boulders.

Lying on my back, panting, it was some time before I noticed the Towers. Not since our first view of them had they appeared so clearly and free of cloud. The skyline looked more like Manhattan than mountains. The lines of the peaks seemed too perpendicular and unbroken to have been created naturally. I half expected to see glass lifts moving up and down the angular corners of the Central Tower.

Frantically I searched the face, unable to locate familiar features. I tried a more methodical approach, following our line up from the glacier. I could see no trace of Paul or Noel. For a brief moment I feared the worst and felt my stomach churn. Then something caught my eye.

About halfway up the face, was a grey figure. I had been fooled by size, expecting him to look smaller. As I watched he inched up the red-brown wall while another stood stationary a short distance below. They had made very good progress. It looked as if they had climbed as much as six hundred feet up the most featureless part of our proposed route.

A clattering of stones and a series of curses signalled the arrival of Sean.

'Bloody scree,' he muttered, a look of disgust on his face, Sean threw his rucsac up against the boulder next to mine and sat down, still breathing heavily. 'Have you seen them?'

'Yeah. They're up on that wall above the Scoop.'

After a moment of confusion his eyes focussed on a spot, his face broadening into a huge smile.

'I see them. They've done brilliantly. With any luck, they'll have done the hardest part of the route and it will be easier above.'

Sean stood up and started waving his arms and yelling. 'Yoo-o-w!' Echoes bounced around the Towers and Paine Chico, a much smaller granite tower on our side of the valley. I joined in and our shouts were soon answered by Noel and Paul. The valley filled with sound.

'They're obviously enjoying themselves,' I said. 'Somehow I doubt if I'd be so jolly in the same place.'

Sean stopped waving and for a moment looked thoughtful. 'I guess we'll find out tomorrow.'

Sean's caution made me feel uneasy. Noel and Paul looked highly vulnerable on the vast granite wall. Tomorrow we would be in the same position. The thought was worrying, but rather than dwell on it, I shouldered my rucsac and set off again.

Gently-angled granite slabs, which looked as though they had only recently surfaced from the retreating glacier, led across to a huge boss of rock which split the Torres Glacier into two forks – one running under the Central Tower, the other further across the valley towards Paine Chico. I paused beneath the strange buttress of rock, surrounded by a sea of ice on three sides, and looked up. Noel and Paul were already on their way down. I watched them taking turns to descend the ropes above the portaledges.

On the lower part of the glacier the fresh snow had melted away, and I moved easily over the hard base, but higher up I came to deep wet snow and was glad of the line of tracks left by Noel and Paul. All around there was evidence of the season's changing. Below the slabs I could hear meltwater percolating down from above.

After a final check of my harness, I started the laborious climb up the ropes. The jumars which clamped around the rope and slid up, but which locked with any downward pull, were now very familiar. I built up a rhythm, sliding first the top jumar up the rope and stepping up in a stirrup of tape that hung from it. The second jumar, connected to my harness at my waist, slid up the rope as I stepped up, and when I slumped back on to my harness, it would take my weight, allowing me to move my first jumar up the rope again.

To keep myself going and maintain a steady progress, I played counting games. My mind drifted in and out of a fantasy world, interrupted at the end of each section of rope. Now and again there would be a sickening downward jolt of the rope as it settled over a small edge above, snapping me back to reality and sending my heart racing. The jerks always worried me and were constant reminders of our total reliance on the line of ropes we had fixed to the rock, leaving a nagging doubt about their safety. I knew that the ropes, when weighted with our bodies, could easily sever over one of the many sharp edges of granite, and, with constant swaying across the rough rock in the wind, sections could fray. Each jolt downwards on the rope produced the momentary fear that it had parted, starting the long brutal fall down the face to the glacier below.

High above, the figures of Noel and Paul were now clearly visible, abseiling down the ropes in the steep corner beneath the portaledges. I followed their bounding downward motion, much faster than my slow upward one. By the time I reached the second belay, a mere three hundred feet above the glacier, they were only a hundred feet away. I decided to wait for them.

It was Noel who first came sliding down towards me. He looked very pleased with himself.

'Ah, Mr Yates! Sorry to have kept you waiting. Happy New Year.' His words came gushing out, although his face looked tired and drawn.

'And a happy New Year to you, Noel. You've done well.'

'Yes, the climbing's been okay, but bloody hard though.' Noel's grin broadened. 'We've had a few falls.'

I have fallen many times while climbing, and have been lucky to escape injury. The falls themselves had not even been bad experiences, but the moments running up to them were all filled with a dreadful fear of the inevitable. Here was a man who seemed to relish the event.

'Paul took a flier,' Noel continued.

'Is he all right?'

'He's fine. A piece of gear ripped out at the top of the Scoop. He fell about forty feet before something held him. I'm the one with the injury.'

'What happened to you?'

'He landed on my head.' Noel was laughing. 'Hurt my neck a bit.'

Sean was nearing the belay from below and Paul was waiting at the next one up. We were causing a bottleneck.

'Okay, Noel, I'd better go. I'll see you in a couple of days' time, if the weather holds out, and sooner if it doesn't.'

I soon regained my jumaring rhythm and moved swiftly up the rope towards Paul. The slabs had changed out of all recognition since we had retreated down in the storm over a week before. The deep covering of powder snow, sheets of ice and buried ropes had gone, to be replaced by dry rock and patches of firm wet snow. It made the job of climbing the ropes much easier, and before long I was approaching Paul's stance.

He, like Noel, looked relaxed and happy, but his old-looking face had aged a few more years. It was not much of an advertisement for what we were doing.

'I hear you took a bit of a lob,' I called out as I got near the belay.

'Oh, it was nothing. Just a bit of gear ripping out.'

Paul spoke in a quiet modest tone, but the experiences of the previous few days had not left him completely unmoved. He looked proud and happy.

'It's wild up there, Simes. Did you see the condors?'

'Yeah, they're beautiful, aren't they?'

'Yesterday they were with us for hours, soaring in circles. Sometimes they were only twenty or thirty feet away, watching our every move. They're just amazing.'

I felt a little envious. They had been lucky to see the birds at such close quarters.

'Oh, well. With a bit of luck they'll be around tomorrow and we'll get to see them. What about the climbing?'

Paul's distant gaze dissolved, but he took a long time before replying.

'It's thin.'

With great care I clipped into the belay and removed my jumars from the rope, contorting myself to reach over Paul and clip them on to the next rope. Once I was safe, I turned to face him.

'Have a good rest. You've deserved it. I'll see you in a few days.'

'Yeah, see you Simes.'

For once it was actually pleasant going up the ropes, not cold, snowing or windy. The sun had shone all day, and although our side of the mountain, facing east, received little of it, the air was noticeably warmer. Climbing up the ropes, I could even take time to appreciate our dramatic surroundings. To my sides and above, huge pillars of orange granite towered up, soaring cracklines running unbroken into the cloud above. Grey scarred rock hung on the vast brown walls and beneath enormous roofs, signs of previous rockfalls, a reminder of the forces of nature and the pull of gravity. It was a climber's paradise, an adventure playground of epic proportions. I felt lucky to be in such a place, and a peace that comes from knowing you are doing the right thing.

I made short work of the remaining climb up to the portaledge camp, dumping my heavy rucsac into the snow next to one of our kitbags with a sigh of relief. The camp was now beginning to look lived in. The patch of snow left under the ledges was stained with patches of urine and discarded drinks. Kitbags hung everywhere, like cocoons, on thin strands of rope.

Sifting through one of our bags, I found our hanging gas

stove and filled the pan with snow. Once the stove was lit I could relax.

Slumping on the ledge, I rolled a cigarette and gazed at the Pampas to the east. The shadows were lengthening now in the golden glow of the early evening light. The clouds that had hung round the summits of the towers had almost disappeared, along with the breeze. It was a perfect evening.

Time passed quickly, the calm pierced only by the quiet purring of the stove. In these conditions even the route above did not seem daunting. I was able to look at the rope above the camp, its thin white cord dropping freely down an under-cut wall for nearly three hundred feet, without feeling any dread. I looked forward to the morning, to reaching the others' high point and getting on to some new ground.

Sean's face was flushed from the exertion when he arrived at the camp, sweat dripping from his hair beneath the front of his helmet. He paused on the rope just a few feet from the belay and grinned.

'It's beautiful, man! Just beautiful.'

'It sure is,' I agreed. 'Grab a seat. The brew's on its way.'

For a long time we sat in perfect silence, gazing at the vast panorama, lost in our own thoughts, until the boiling stove snapped us out of our respective trances. As I made the drinks Sean started rifling through the Spanish kitbags.

'What are you looking for?' I asked. 'Goodies to go with the brew?'

Sean's torso completely disappeared into one of the largest orange bags. After a few writhing movements, accompanied by muffled grunts, he reappeared.

'No! I was after this.'

Slowly and deliberately he pulled his arms out of the bag, clutching a large radio. Two wires hung from the battery compartment in the back. He returned to the kitbag and pulled out a battery. He connected it to the radio, and turned it on. The machine crackled fiercely as Sean fiddled with the tuning, quickly hitting a station where a deep-voiced DJ momentarily enthused in Spanish before the air filled with music. A salsa band. Sean gyrated on the spot, wriggling his hips in time with the music. I burst into laughter.

'Radio Natales!' he proudly announced. 'Paul told me they'd found a radio, but I thought he was having me on. Those Spanish guys certainly liked their comforts.' Waving his hands like a Shakespearean actor, he pointed to another Spanish kitbag. 'And in this bag we have our colour TV, and over here our microwave. I couldn't consider climbing a wall of this size without them. Oh, and this, of course, is the kitchen sink.'

We both dissolved into fits of childish giggling. The radio reunited us with the real world, now quite removed from our own. Beyond our tower of rock, the focus of our attentions, people were still going about their lives, working, eating and sleeping. The radio simply reminded us of where we were and what we were trying to achieve. It suddenly seemed quite ridiculous.

After eating, we climbed on to our portaledges and lay in our sleeping bags. As darkness fell, lights started to flicker invitingly from the isolated sheep farms out on the Pampas. I stared at them, almost envious of the limitless space and freedom they seemed to offer, the luxuries of proper beds and decent food. Deep down though, I knew that after a short time I would find the space and luxuries stifling and boring. I would need another challenge.

I rolled over to face Sean lying on his own portaledge, a few feet above and to the side of me.

'What time should I set the alarm for tomorrow morning?'

'Round about dawn, I suppose.'

'What time is that?'

'It's light by six-thirty.'

'I'll set it for about an hour before that.'

'Make it six-thirty. The days are plenty long enough at the moment. Besides' – Sean paused and a mischievous smile spread across his face – 'we wouldn't want to break habits of a lifetime.'

'Quite!'

FOUR

〰

Taking
the
Strain

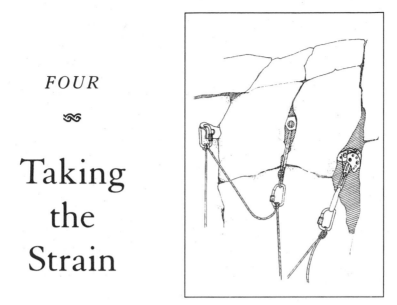

I made the first hot drink of the day without leaving the comfort of my sleeping bag. Then it was necessary to start the laborious routine of preparing for the day's climbing. Out of the sleeping bag, quickly on with some more clothes. Put on helmet. I ran through the list slowly and deliberately in my mind, careful not to forget anything. Lastly, plastic boots. I always took great care with these, having heard many stories of epic retreats from mountains caused by dropping them. Sean followed his own routine and our actions proceeded in a careful slow motion, limited by our unusual location. Finally we could both leave our portaledges.

A further time-consuming process had to be completed from the confined space of the small snow-covered ledge beneath the portaledges before climbing could begin. Going to the toilet – never a pleasant business in the mountains – was awkward and dangerous here. A makeshift rope harness needed to be looped under each arm and around the chest before the main harness was removed from around the waist and one could lean backwards out over the abyss below in a squatting position. I found the idea of falling while going to the toilet highly embarrassing and so always took great care.

There was little to pack for the day as we would be returning in the evening. I stuffed a spare jacket, a water bottle and some chocolate into my rucsac. At last I was ready to set off up the ropes.

'D'you want to go first, Sean?' I asked nervously.

'No, you get going. I'm not quite ready.'

'Okay. You can lead the first pitch. I'll sort out the ropes for you when I get to the high point.'

'Fine. See you up there.'

With some apprehension I shuffled along the ledge and clipped my jumars on to the rope that soared up the overhanging wall above. The rope had been tied down to prevent it lashing around in the wind. I untied it so that it would be possible to abseil back down, but now the slack rope hung even further out from the wall.

I slid my jumars up the rope until all the slack had been taken in and paused. The moment I had been silently dreading had now arrived. Taking a deep breath, I let my weight hang on the rope and, closing my eyes, stepped off the ledge. I pendulumed out into space off to the right of the ledges and hung there about fifteen feet from the wall. I felt quite pleased – the rope had held and the swing hadn't been as frightening as I expected. Given another location, say hanging from the branch of a tree above a shallow stream, it might have been enjoyable, but with a thousand-foot-drop or more to the glacier below, I could not think in such terms. Taking deliberate care not to look down, I quickly started jumaring up the rope.

It took many minutes of gentle climbing up the free-hanging rope for the fear to subside, leaving me with my usual nagging doubts about the safety of the rope which, as always, seemed far too thin and fragile. Higher up, the rope crept back towards the rock again. Being able to touch the rock lessened the feeling of exposure, giving psychological comfort if little real assistance. Eventually I reached a belay, clipped into it and was then able to relax at last with my weight on a metal peg securely embedded in a horizontal crack. For the first time, I looked down. The view on to the sweeping slabs and glacier below was both exhilarating and heart-stopping. Although I was only a hundred feet above it, the portaledge camp already looked tiny. Catching Sean's attention by waving my arm, I shouted into the void.

'Start climbing!'

'Okay, I'm on my way!' drifted up on the slight breeze.

The two short sentences mingled into a brief series of echoes, that reverberated across the Torres Glacier before abruptly dying away.

The next rope length passed quickly and I found myself stepping up on to ledges at the top of the shattered pillar. It was as high as I had been before.

Above, the rope soared once more, up a gently overhanging shallow corner – a pale grey line of weakness, scything through an otherwise featureless sweep of orange granite. We had already given it a name – the Scoop. There wasn't a ledge in sight.

Fortunately, Noel and Paul had fixed our thickest and strongest rope on this section of the climb. Unlike the one below, it did not stretch when I put my weight on to it. I felt confident the rope would not break, letting me dwell instead on the unnerving exposure.

Moving smoothly up the rope, I marvelled at the difficulty of the climbing Noel and Paul had accomplished. I now understood what Paul meant when he said the climbing had been thin.

In the back of the Scoop was a hair-line crack, just a few millimetres wide. It was the only feature they would have been able to climb. I knew what that must have entailed. Metal pegs delicately placed and hammered into the tiny weakness, then gently tested with a firm pull before stepping up on them. Such climbing is very insecure, each peg placement barely holding the climber's weight. If a peg pulls out, the resulting fall is likely to be long, as more pull out below. Only a good solidly placed peg clipped into the rope would stop the fall. In the feature I was now looking at there were few such placements.

At the top of the Scoop the rock bulged dramatically and the shallow corner gradually petered out. In the confines of the corner the rock hemmed me in, giving me a sense of security. I now found myself once more following the rope up a gently impending wall with nothing but space on either side and – more disturbing – a huge emptiness below.

I was now six hundred feet above the portaledge camp, although it was impossible to see it, the bulging rock obscuring it from view. I stared down the clean cut corner leading up to the portaledges which, from my viewpoint, looked quite easy-angled. The snow-covered slabs now appeared flat and it was hard to distinguish them from the glacier nearly two thousand feet below. Never before had I been in such an overwhelming situation. The seemingly infinite space produced an intense feeling of freedom. In many ways the strange and surreal world that I was now in did not feel natural – it was too simple, just rock and sky – but it was exciting, and I felt relaxed and comfortable. The only reminder of the other real world below was the thin thread of rope on which I was hanging. It stretched to the ground, to that other world, and allowed us to return whenever we chose. It was a lifeline in many different ways – some real and some symbolic. That was why, at the start of the day, I had been so scared that the rope would sever. I did not want to leave that other world, either physically or mentally, merely to escape from it for a while.

Above the bulging wall the angle eased to just off vertical and it was possible to see higher above. Just forty or fifty feet above, the rope ended in a cluster of climbing hardware, ropes and the black haulbag. I put on a spurt of speed up the last of the fixed rope, excited by the prospect of going higher through our own efforts.

As I clipped into the belay, I saw that Sean was still some way behind. The early morning sun was now shining square on to the rock and felt warm on my face, even though the air had not yet lost its chill. I relished the warm rays and turned my head from one side to the other, soaking them up, knowing they would not last long – we got direct sun for just the few hours after dawn. By the middle of the day, I could only look out enviously beyond the enormous shadow cast by the Central

Tower to the sunlight shining on the glacier and the mountains on the other side of the valley.

The thin crack continued up the wall to a large cleft, a prominent feature on our chosen line, and one we had rather morbidly named the Coffin. It all looked climbable – there were cracks, grooves and corners. What we dreaded was reaching a section of blank rock, which it would only be possible to climb by drilling holes and placing expansion bolts in them. We had no more than a handful of bolts with us. A blank section over thirty feet high would stop us.

The rope below came under tension and started to flex. Sean was on his way up the last section and I hurried to sort out the gear so that it was ready for him to lead the next pitch. When he came into view, gradually making his way round the bulge below, his red face looked a picture of concentration. I finished untangling the ropes as he made a last effort, stopping just below me. He hung there limply on the rope, shaking his head.

'Did you enjoy that?' I asked.

Sean shook his head faster. 'We must be right off our rockers, doing this!'

'You took your time,' I said.

'Yes, well, my feet were cold.'

I was surprised. Ever since the early morning, when we left the portaledges, my feet had remained warm.

'How come?' I asked.

'I left my plastic boots at the bottom of the ropes yesterday.'

I was amazed. I had noticed the day before that Sean had been climbing in his canvas walking boots, but assumed he had his plastic mountaineering boots in his rucsac. First his gloves and now his boots, I thought: two elementary and serious mistakes in the space of days.

'Well, that wasn't very clever.' It was all I could think of to say.

After a few minutes the sweat stopped pouring down Sean's face and he tied into the ends of the ropes. I started passing him the climbing hardware from the haulbag and watched his shoulders sag as he hung sling after sling of glittering ironmongery around his neck – pegs for hammering into cracks, nuts (metal wedges on loops of wire to slide into constrictions in cracks), and Friends (devices with four spring-loaded cams mounted on a metal stem: by pulling a trigger to compress the cams, the Friend can be inserted into cracks; releasing the trigger allows it to expand and grip the inside of the crack). All the gear hung from dozens of karabiners, necessary to clip each piece to the rope once it was placed in the rock. At last he was ready.

'Have you got me?' he said calmly with a look of intense concentration.

'Yes, I'm watching you,' I assured him as he left the belay.

However I tried, I could not get comfortable. Sean's progress was slow and I wished he would hurry up. Pressure from the leg loops of my harness made my lower legs go numb and a dull ache started at the base of my spine. All I could do was continually to shift my weight, giving temporary relief for a small area of pain or numbness. The longer I hung, the more frequent my shifting and fidgeting became.

Sean was making heavy work of it above. I knew it had been a long time since he had done any of this style of climbing and his movements looked unfamiliar and strained. I struggled to remain patient and control the growing feeling of resentment. I knew that I would not be able to climb much faster. Sean must have sensed my growing anxiety for he looked down apologetically, his face now bright red again.

'Sorry I'm taking so long. I'm a bit rusty with this sort of climbing.'

'That's all right,' I lied. 'Take as long as you need.'

Once Sean was out of sight, I tried to entertain myself by staring at the crystals in the rock, imagining faces or strange patterns, playing with karabiners, inspecting the weave of the rope's sheath. My mind drifted into elaborate day-dreams, only broken by the need to feed out more rope or shift my body yet again. A breeze chilled the air, adding cold to the list of my discomforts. I put on a pair of gloves and huddled against the rock. At last Sean shouted down that he was safe.

To my great relief, there was now actually something to which I could give my full attention. I attached the haul-bag to the end of one of Sean's ropes, then slowly he took in the slack in all the ropes and gave the signal for me to start moving.

How good it was to be jumaring again, to feel my blood circulating freely and to exchange cold for warmth. I paused only to remove from the rock the pieces of equipment Sean had placed. As I approached him, Sean was manoeuvring in a shallow corner to find a comfortable position in which to belay me while I led the pitch above. It didn't look as if he was having much luck. Eventually he settled with his back against one wall and his feet bridged out on the other.

The way above was brutally obvious. A large flake of rock led into a shallow corner on the left and then ran up to a large recess. It was broader in the middle than at either end. The whole feature gently overhung and had the appearance of a giant lift housing, although the name we had already given it now seemed even more apt. The recess matched the shape of a coffin almost perfectly. All it needed was a lid. I took a deep breath and carried on up the rope until I was just below Sean.

'That was a good lead, Sean. Well done.'

'Cheers. I was struggling a bit at first though.'

'Yeah, I noticed.'

'I was getting it together by the top of the pitch,' Sean said in a mockingly defensive way.

'It's okay. I'm not getting at you.'

I knew that rushing was out of the question anyway. It was much better to be slow and safe than hurry and risk a fall, and while Sean's slowness sometimes annoyed me, there was no one with whom I felt safer while climbing.

Leaving the belay was difficult. I needed to be above Sean to reach the flake of rock that led across to the Coffin. The only way to reach it was to clamber awkwardly over the top of him, while he tried to move to one side. It was impossible to avoid treading on him, producing groans of complaint, before my hands sank into the large holds at the back of the flake and I was able to pull myself above him.

71

Once on the flake I had to move quickly and free-climb into the corner ten feet away. In normal circumstances, this would have presented a problem. The handholds were enormous, but having got used to aid-climbing, relying completely on my own body seemed strangely unfamiliar. The weight of equipment made me feel cumbersome and strength quickly drained from my arms. Realising that I could not hang on for long, I lunged to the left, and in a series of rapid ape-like movements, swung across the flake, stopping at the end beneath the corner. A race was now on. I needed to get a piece of equipment into the crack above and clip into it before my strength ran out. A fall would send me plummeting back towards Sean and smashing into the corner beneath him. It was not a prospect I relished. I selected a nut and tried to place it in the crack above with my right hand. It was too large and would not fit. My left arm buckled under the increased strain and my hand uncurled from behind the flake. I put my right hand back on the flake just as the left arm finally gave out. Shaking it vigorously to speed up recovery, I started to panic. My right arm was now losing strength fast and I had to change arms once more. Selecting a smaller nut, I reached up and placed it in the crack. Fortunately it fitted and, with much fumbling, I managed to clip my rope on to the nut. Badly frightened, I stared at Sean.

'Take in, Sean. Quickly!' My voice quivered as I spoke.

While the slack in the rope was taken in, I hung weakly from the flake of rock. It seemed to take an eternity before the rope came tight at my waist, and when it did, I unashamedly slumped on to it and dangled limply, feet off the rock, panting furiously. As my anxiety subsided I felt a buzz at overcoming the short-lived crisis.

After a brief rest I continued up the crack, happy to be hanging on pieces of equipment again rather than my arms. At the top of the corner I peered round into the Coffin. It had cracks in both of its corners. The one nearest me looked the easier to climb. Moving round into it proved to be straight-forward. The crack was now wide enough to take Friends, and these I hoped would allow me to move more swiftly. With their trigger-controlled variable size, they were much easier to place and remove than the single-size nuts. Unlike nuts, which held through being wedged into a constriction in a crack, the expanding cams of Friends worked well in parallel-sided cracks, such as the one I was now climbing. I selected one that looked the right size from the slings hanging round my neck. Unfortunately it was old and, due to wear and tear, a wire from the trigger to the one of the cams had broken. The device no longer opened and closed as it should. Despite the amount of equipment I was carrying, there were only two others which fitted into the crack. I climbed by placing one above me, then stepping up on a sling clipped to it and repeating the move with the second Friend before removing the lower one. The leap-frogging technique proved very efficient and I made rapid progress, but as I needed both the devices to climb the crack, it was not possible to leave one behind clipped into the rope to stop me should I fall. I soon found myself way above the last nut clipped to the rope at the bottom of the Coffin. The higher I went above it, the further I would fall if I made a mistake.

The rock quality suddenly changed. The clean-sided crack became rounded, soft and crumbly. The cams of the Friends started to bite into the rock, which crumbled as I placed my weight on them. I knew that if the cams opened too wide, the Friend would pull out, sending me hurtling into the space below. Yet, despite the obvious danger, a feeling of calm and confidence came over me. Although it was not rational, I felt sure that nothing bad was going to happen.

The feeling was familiar. It had overcome me many times before, usually when I was alone, climbing without a rope on summer evenings on gritstone crags in the Peak District just outside Sheffield, and also on days of ice-climbing in Scotland. The feeling had rarely occurred in the mountains though. Perhaps their obvious seriousness had prevented it.

One winter in Scotland I had stood beneath Minus One Gully, the hardest gully climb on the north face of Ben Nevis, and decided to climb it. The conditions were good; the whole face was plastered in an icy white coating and the sky was almost clear. A few benign clouds swirled around the summit as I started up the thousand-foot gully.

The climbing was near perfect in the lower part and my crampons bit firmly into the plastic white ice. With a single blow, each of my ice-axe placements held just as easily. Even though the ice was vertical in places, I felt completely in control. Soon I was hundreds of feet up the gully, entering a small cave, knowing that leaving it would be the hardest part of the climb.

From here the way ahead looked difficult. A horizontal series of small blobs of water-ice, glued to the vertical rock of the left wall of the cave, offered the only escape. I studied them briefly and then set off. Although less than an inch deep, I managed to place my axes in the small patches of ice which rocked in the tiny holes as I placed my weight on them. It was hard to find anywhere to plant my feet, and occasionally my crampons skidded off the rock below. My arms started to tire. Ten feet along the traverse I knew I was completely committed and too tired to turn back. The patches of ice were getting progressively thinner.

At the end of the wall was a final smear of ice, less than half an inch thick. I placed an axe in it and moved across, quickly thrusting in the other axe as I went. The axe placements were just above my face, and I stared at the single teeth on the tips of the axe blades as they bit into the very thin plate of ice which was scarred with cracks radiating out from the two holes. If the ice broke, I would fall almost certainly to my death – although the thought never crossed my mind. I felt sure that the thin shattered piece of ice would hold my weight, so I removed my left axe to make the next placement. The remaining axe wobbled from side to side as I battled to hold it steady.

The wall ended abruptly in an outward-facing corner, which I needed to turn, though I could not see round it. My right arm was becoming dangerously tired. I put my left arm around the corner and probed with the tip of my axe. It touched something solid. I pulled the axe back and took a swing. The dull resonating thud assured me that the axe had embedded into some good ice and I swung round the corner and hammered the other axe in as hard as I could. The danger had passed.

As I climbed up the vertical ice above I started thinking: *you could have died there, Simon. You could die now if your axes rip out, or that piece of ice comes away*. The thoughts did not bother me. Overwhelmed with a sense of absolute freedom, I was floating up the climb. My movements seemed perfect. What I was doing felt completely natural. In a way, it was a feeling of supreme confidence, but it went beyond that. I was concerned about nothing; the thought of death, though very real, held no fear whatever for me.

Later, after I had completed the climb and reached the summit, I ran down an easy gully and snow slope, screaming with delight, not stopping until I reached the hut at the bottom of the face. It was only eleven in the morning and I lay on my back, soaking up the weak winter sun, contemplating another climb. Looking up at the mountain face, it seemed different then, cold, hostile and forbidding.

When I got up to leave I took one last look at the complex of buttresses, ridges and gullies, carefully picking out the line of my route to the Ben Nevis summit. A lump came into my throat. The emotion that I had controlled so well on the mountain suddenly welled up inside me and tears poured down my cheeks, yet at the same time I was laughing, a little at first, then hysterically. In that instant, I knew I had overstepped the fine line between confidence and carelessness and in doing so had gambled with my life. Fortunately, I had won. As I turned to go my legs buckled and I fell to the ground. Quickly I got up again, but it seemed impossible to co-ordinate my limbs properly. It was all I could do to follow the easy well-worn path back to the valley.

FIVE

∽

Learning
the
Ropes

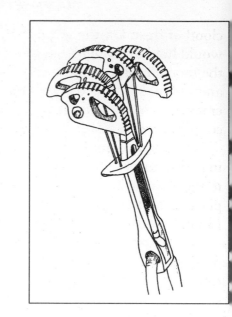

High up in the Coffin I watched each Friend with a morbid curiosity as I stepped up and put my full weight on to it. Each upward movement was like pulling the trigger in a game of Russian roulette. The crack continued to widen and the Friend placements became even more insecure, allowing nagging doubts to creep into my mind. The confidence with which I had started to climb the crumbling crack ebbed away. It had become a simple matter of survival. There was no possibility of climbing down the way I had just come up. My only option was to keep going, up to where the crack narrowed again, where it would be possible to place a secure piece of equipment and leave it clipped on to the rope to safeguard further progress. All I could do until then was to hope the devices – now holding by the very tips of their cams – did not rip away from the wall, which seemed more and more likely as the crack grew wider.

Approaching the widest part of the crack, I paused to wipe away sweat that was dripping from my face and oozing from my hands. The Friend slid all too easily into the crack above me, with only the very tips of its four metal cams touching the sides. I gave it a gentle pull. The cams dug momentarily into the crumbling granite before the whole thing ripped out in a small cloud of dust. On the second attempt it held. I doubted that it would hold my weight, but there seemed little point in delaying the moment of truth. I put my foot in the sling hanging from it and very gently pulled myself upright. The Friend slipped in the crack and my heart leapt as its cams bit into the rock and held a couple of inches lower. A wave of panic subsided.

In a series of quick movements I followed the now diminishing crack until I reach a spot where I was able to slide a nut into it above a constriction and pull it down to wedge it firmly in place. Once the nut was in the crack, with the rope clipped to it, I knew I was safe at last. I let out a small scream of delight.

The climbing above was difficult and demanding but not dangerous. At the top of the Coffin the crack that I had been following petered out, forcing me to move to the other side of the strange feature. The swing across was gut-wrenching with the enormous recess dropping away in a concave arc beneath me.

A shout came up from below, echoing around the walls, pillars and corners of the surrounding rock.

'Ten feet!'

The simple message told me how much rope remained. I would have to find a belay very shortly. A small roof about two feet across blocked my exit from the Coffin. As I swung out across it Sean came into view again and I waved at his tiny figure. It was just possible to make out the smile on his face as he waved back.

My position was now spectacular as I dangled from the underside of the roof, peering down through my legs at the orange, grey and brown sheets of granite sweeping down to the slabs far below. Directly beneath me, I could make out the patch of snow, studded with tiny footprints and stains under the portaledge camp. It looked a very long way down.

Much to my surprise, a few feet above the roof I found a small shelf – the perfect spot for a belay. Unfortunately the shelf was not big enough, nor sufficiently level, to sit on, but with a little cunning I managed to construct a belay just above it. By tying myself to the belay on carefully measured lengths of rope, it was possible to get part of my backside on to the sloping shelf, taking some of my weight off the harness, which by now was cutting painfully into my hips and thighs. Feeling very pleased with myself, I sat facing out, taking in the rope and wriggling my legs, which tingled, as blood flowed freely around them for the first time in hours.

'Okay, Sean. Cliiimb!' I yelled into the void.

Sean had obviously been waiting for my signal, for he started climbing almost immediately. I alternated my time between hauling up our big black kitbag, which spun on the end of the rope like a disorientated spider, and staring out into the abundance of space. As Sean drew closer I watched him, hanging a good five feet out from the rock, inching his way up the rope, a stern look of concentration on his face.

With the extra height came further views. To the west, it was now possible to see more huge granite walls in the Valley Frances, and I could look down on the range of foothills to the east of our base camp, though the deep notch between the Central and South Towers was still tantalisingly blank. I knew that around there somewhere were the impressive walls of Cathedral and the Fortress, almost as big as the wall we were on now. There was absolutely nowhere I would rather have been. When Sean arrived, he looked as if he was enjoying himself.

'Well led,' he said. 'How are we doing for time?'

'Good grief!' I exclaimed. 'It's nearly six o'clock. What do you want to do?'

'I'll carry on for a little while longer. Then we'd better go down. I don't want to get back to the portaledges too late. We've got another long day tomorrow.'

He made perfect sense. Although it didn't get dark until eleven, it would take a couple of hours to melt water and cook, and we then needed a good night's sleep.

'That's fine by me,' I said.

Sean sorted out the equipment and moved slowly out of sight up the wall above. As the rope inched through the belay plate, I sat watching the shadows of the Towers lengthening across the glacier below and up the cliffs opposite. The wind began to feel cold. I put on my spare jacket and gloves and began to shake my legs again, but I was soon shivering. There was little to do but pay out the rope and silently hope that Sean would soon call it a day. After what seemed like an eternity, with half the rope still remaining, I heard him shout.

'I'm coming down. I'll just make the rope safe.'

Feeling unpleasantly cold, with numb hands and feet, I willed Sean to hurry up as the sound of metal pegs being hammered into the rock drifted down from above.

'Safe!' he called finally.

'Okay, I'm off now,' I yelled back, as I put my descender on to the rope beneath the belay. Within seconds I had clipped it into my harness, untied from my ends of the ropes and launched myself down the Coffin.

My joy at moving again evaporated as I found myself hanging in space just a few feet below the belay. When climbing up, I had been looking at the rock in front of me or just above, but as I slid down the rope it was necessary to look down all the time at the sickening drop below. I felt my stomach tighten as I let the rope through the descender in small bursts, accelerating until I was scared of losing my grip, then hastily slowing down.

At the bottom of the Coffin I reached the first belay, which heightened my anxiety. In order to swap the descender on to the next rope, it was necessary to clip a sling attached to my harness into the belay and hang from it while completing the change-over. The manoeuvre, though simple, always frightened me. If I clipped the sling wrongly to the belay, or failed to clip the descender back on to my harness correctly, I would fall. I checked every stage of the process very carefully, well aware of the large number of mountaineering deaths caused by mistakes while abseiling.

The evening was now perfect. The wind had dropped and the sky was clear. The cliffs opposite glowed a deep orange in the last of the day's sun. Nervously I made my way down the wall, occasionally catching glimpses of Sean above.

Once inside the Scoop I felt more secure and able to abseil faster. Soon I reached the bottom, with just the rope hanging down the overhanging wall to descend to reach the camp. I had not been looking forward to this last abseil, but the promise of food and drink was now uppermost in my mind. I completed the changeover quickly and started sliding down the final rope. At first this gave me no problems, but as I moved further out from the rock I started spinning, first one way, then the other, my view alternating between the grey wall of granite and the vast expanse of the Pampas. The motion made me feel giddy, but I was determined not to allow the terror I had felt going up the rope in the morning a chance to return. I let the rope through the descender quickly and soon found myself bouncing on a loop of rope just above the snow slope at the side of the camp. Pulling myself across to the portaledges, I let out a long breath and the tension evaporated with it. The day's climbing was over.

By the time Sean arrived, the stove was humming and a much-needed brew was well on the way. He looked tired but relaxed as he climbed up the short slope into the camp.

'How's it going?' I greeted him.

'Oh, all right, I guess. Still a bit slow.'

'Don't be hard on yourself,' I said mockingly. 'We've made good progress today. At this rate, we might even finish by Easter.'

Later, as I drifted off to sleep, I hoped that we would not encounter too much more difficult climbing and that, if the weather remained good, we would soon be making an attempt on the summit.

*

The alarm heralding a new day seemed unduly harsh. I felt like going back to sleep, but instead coaxed my tired, stiff body back into action. A quick inspection of my hips, which were particularly sore, revealed large blue-green bruises from hanging so long in my climbing harness, and it took all my willpower to get up and face another day's climbing.

We ambled through our early morning routine. It was more than an hour later than the previous day when Sean finally started jumaring up the rope above the camp. As I watched his

The east faces of the South, Central and North Towers of Paine
in Chilean Patagonia. (Photo: Sean Mayne Smith)

Paul Pritchard on the lower slopes of the climb, and Sean Smith following the
corner that led to the portaledge camp. (Photos: Simon Yates)

Left: Noel Craine on Christmas Day at the portaledge camp. (Photo: Smith)

Below: Simon Yates, reluctant to leave the comfort of his portaledge. (Photo: Paul Pritchard)

Right: Simon jumaring above the portaledge camp. (Photo: Pritchard)

Below right: Paul following the top part of the Scoop. (Photo: Noel Craine)

Left: Simon entering the Coffin.
(Photo: Smith)

Below left: Looking down through Simon's legs at Sean sitting on the first ledge in over a thousand feet of climbing. (Photo: Yates)

Right: Returning to the portaledge camp at the end of a day's climbing above. (Photo: Yates)

Below: Hanneke Steenmetz with Paul outside the hut at base camp. (Photo: Pritchard)

Left: Sean entering the chimney beneath the top bivouac shortly before he fell. (Photo: Yates)

Below left: Simon and Sean sit out the storm at the top bivouac. (Photo: Pritchard)

Right: The forest around the base camp. (Photo: Yates)

low: At the Maritimo restaurant in Puerto Natales - Paul, Sean, teve Hayward, Noel and Simon. spite our dishevelled appearance after the storm, the proprietor recognised us at once from this earlier visit.' (Photo: Yates)

Above: Looking north-west from the summit of the Central Tower towards the Patagonian Ice Cap. (Photo: Smith)

Right: Paul and Sean on the summit of the Central Tower. (Photo: Pritchard)

Below: The big, bad Patagonian sky. (Photo: Smith)

slow, stiffened movements it was obvious we would not make as much progress as on the day before.

I followed in a similar condition, my tiredness having one beneficial effect: I no longer felt bothered by my surroundings and moved up the rope like a zombie. Even the changeovers produced little anxiety. Several hours more work awaited above and climbing the ropes seemed not much more than a strange form of commuting.

Once up to the sloping ledge at the top of the Coffin I settled into belaying Sean as he completed the pitch he had started the night before. When I followed, it was easy to see why he had been taking his time. The crack above my stance had thinned and in places looked almost blind, forcing him to hammer thin metal pegs into the seam. He had had to make many such placements. They stretched up as far as I could see. It was only when I got near the end of the rope that I saw him sitting comfortably on a two-foot-wide ledge, the ropes neatly coiled beside him.

'You jammy sod!' I shouted up.

'Yeah, not a bad spot, is it?' he replied.

It was the first place where we could sit in over a thousand feet of climbing. As I stretched out on the ledge next to Sean I felt my aches and pains gradually subside. The ledge, although only two feet wide by about twelve feet long, felt much bigger, such was the freedom of movement it allowed. For a few minutes I wallowed in the luxury of the small horizontal world. It felt like a significant point, a benchmark, the first sign that the climbing was easing and would be more straightforward above.

Unfortunately the feeling was short-lived. I had great difficulty getting off the ledge, up a small bulging wall, and the climbing up thin seams above was some of the hardest I had led. I looked down through my legs at Sean with some envy. He lay reclining on the ledge, having made the coils of rope into a pillow. Eventually the seams gave way to a more definite crack leading up to a deep chimney, and the climbing became easier.

While coping with the hard section, I had failed to notice the worsening weather. The ever-present wind had steadily become more fierce and a veil of grey cloud descended around us. Small pellets of snow were now falling and ricocheting down the rock. The roofs and chimney above gave me some protection from the elements, but down on the exposed ledge Sean was now suffering. I watched as he struggled to put on a waterproof jacket which flapped and billowed like a sail in the wind.

There seemed little point in carrying on. I, for one, did not want our shift on the mountain to end in an epic struggle to get down in a storm. Besides, I felt we had done our bit, and I was already thinking of all the food down in the base camp.

I climbed to the base of the chimney, where it was obvious the ground above would be easier, before shouting down to Sean.

'Shall we call it a day?'

'You bet. My bum is freezing down here.'

It was not long before he disappeared down the rope. I quickly completed the belay, hung the equipment and haul bag from it and set off down after him. Two abseils later the snow stopped and the cloud began to break up. For a brief moment I felt we had been hasty in deciding to go down, but the doubts did not last long. They were soon overcome by the desire for a decent meal and a good night's sleep in the comfort of the forest camp.

Slithering down the last abseil to the portaledge camp, I was surprised to see Noel and Paul. It was only late afternoon and I hadn't expected to see them until I was back in the forest. Noel handed me a welcome brew while Paul filled the stove pan with more snow.

'Ah, wonderful. Thanks,' I said. 'What's brought you up here so soon?'

'We wanted to make an early start tomorrow,' Noel replied. 'Besides,' he continued, 'there's not much to do in the base camp.'

What about eating and sleeping, I thought – and judging by Sean's expression, I wasn't alone. Their keenness had astounded us before, but this seemed altogether extreme.

'Have you brought any decent food with you?' I asked. 'I'm already fed up with pilchards and mash.'

'Well, now you come to mention it, we might have a few goodies with us,' Noel teased. 'We ate so much last night we could hardly walk. Could we, Paul?' Paul nodded, and I felt my mouth filling with saliva.

Paul produced an opened bag of Dulce de Leche from the top of his rucsac. With exaggerated relish, he squeezed a huge dollop of the caramel-like substance on to his index finger and started slowly licking it.

'Hmm, Dulce de Leche,' he muttered. 'We love Dulce, don't we, Noel?'

'You bet,' Noel agreed.

Violent thoughts started entering my head and I was just about to make a snatch for the bag when Paul handed it over.

'Here you go, Simes. How's the climbing?'

I ignored Paul's question, hastily sucking mouthfuls of the thick, sweet fluid straight from the bag. Only when I started to feel sick, did I hand it to Sean and offer Paul a reply.

'We've managed to do another five hundred feet and the ground above looks easier.'

'You reckon?' said Sean. 'It still looked pretty steep to me.'

'Well, still steep,' I replied defensively, 'but there is a good crack to follow.'

'So – what are you saying, Simes? Is it much the same above?' Paul asked slowly and deliberately.

'Yes, but easier.'

'That means we should be able to make a dash for the summit soon,' Noel enthused.

'See what you've started now?' Sean said, grinning at me.

'Look,' I countered. 'We don't have to make any decisions yet, but maybe we should start thinking about it. After another couple of days of fixing rope, we could be quite near.'

'Then again, we might not be,' Sean pointed out, cutting open the bag of Dulce to get at the last of its contents.

Noel was getting visibly excited. 'Let's go for it, as soon as possible,' he said. 'Otherwise I'll have to head back home without even trying for the top.'

'Noel does deserve a chance,' Paul added supportively.

'Steady on,' said Sean. 'We still have the small matter of another couple of thousand feet of climbing before anyone reaches the top.'

'Good point,' I said.

Paul and Noel started to debate between themselves as to how to make the summit attempt. I looked at Sean and raised my hands apologetically before starting to pack my rucsac. A little later, as I shuffled across the ledges to the start of the ropes down, they had even gone as far as deciding what food we would take on the summit attempt.

'Perhaps we should see how the climbing goes and discuss this when we next meet.' I tried and failed to interrupt. 'Ah, sod it. I'll see you in a couple of days!' I shouted at them, as I slid off down the rope.

'See you,' Paul and Noel said together in a brief pause in their conversation.

SIX

〜

New Reso- lution

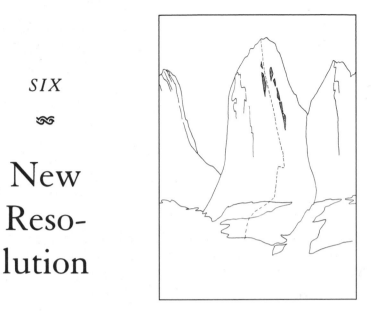

Back in the forest all was calm. In our two days up on the wall in good weather, I had got used to the continual noise of the wind and the mental numbness it caused. The silence under the trees seemed deafening.

The Patagonian summer was now at its most active and vibrant. Even in our short absence, the pale green carpet of plants covering the forest floor had grown a couple of inches higher and flowers were now in abundance. The smell of fresh vegetation hung in the air.

Although the environment was strange and alien, it re- minded me of home. I imagined walking through woods, alive with new growth and birdsong, knee deep in bluebells. For a moment I felt homesick. I was missing out on my favourite time of the year. My confusion did not last long. I soon realised that Britain was in the depths of winter. In climatic terms, we had made a very timely seasonal migration and as a result would be treated to two summers in the one year.

As I crossed the small stream the camp appeared to be empty. I dumped my rucsac in the lean-to and went inside the hut. The place was surprisingly tidy. I cut several pieces of cheese and ate them greedily until my hunger subsided. Hanneke must have heard me in the kitchen because as I wandered out towards her tent she unzipped the flap and stepped out.

'Hi, Simon.' She smiled as she spoke. 'Good climbing?'

'Yes, very good. We're actually making progress.'

'Great,' said Hanneke as a second figure emerged from her tent. I recognised Hanneke's friend immediately as an American, Steve Hayward, whom I had met briefly on our first evening in the Park.

'Hi there,' Steve said as he walked towards me with an outstretched hand.

'And what brings you up here?' I asked. He looked at Hanneke fondly, and they both started laughing.

I liked the laid-back Californian who had completed a new route of his own on the Central Tower just before we arrived. He had given us a lot of useful information, as well as three hundred feet of rope.

With Steve's help, Hanneke had brought up fresh supplies from the town. We were eating an astonishing amount of food and, as usual, had underestimated how much we would need. Her willingness to go back to Puerto Natales for more was a blessing. Without her help we would have had to disrupt our climbing to make the journey ourselves.

Inside the hut, with the fire relighted and a pan of water heating, Steve produced a carton of wine. It was a typically generous gesture and most welcome after two days of stressful activity up on the wall. I felt tired and drank slowly. Despite that, the doubts I had had earlier in the expedition no longer troubled me. I knew that what we were doing was right, although as I stared into my cup of wine I couldn't help seeing some irony in our situation. If we were all that comfortable with what we were doing, why did we spend so much of our rest time drinking?

A series of curses jolted me out of my introspection as the door swung open and Sean hobbled inside.

'Bloody knee's playing up,' he announced while making straight for the cheese.

'Oh, no! Do you think you'll be all right?' I asked,

remembering the start of his knee problem on an expedition in Pakistan two years before.

'Yeah, yeah,' he replied through a mouthful of cheese. 'I'll just have to be careful.'

Although the knee had improved with rest, it still gave Sean trouble after prolonged downhill use. He had even bought a neoprene support and ski poles to help prevent a recurrence. With Noel due to return home shortly, there was suddenly the very real possibility that the team would be reduced to just two climbers. It was not a prospect I relished. Although a team of two would be perfectly capable of finishing the route, it would be very difficult for one person to rescue the other in the event of an accident.

*

I woke late the following morning, feeling dozy and stiff after our recent exertions. As I dragged my aching body out of the sleeping bag I became aware of a change outside. The wind had returned and was rushing over the tree canopy above. When I looked outside, the tops of the Towers were shrouded in thick grey cloud. It would be only a matter of time before rain arrived. I worried that Noel and Paul would already be feeling the brunt of the weather change, but they should already be on their way down and would surely arrive back in the camp later that morning.

After breakfast, Steve prepared to leave, returning to the hut to say his goodbyes. He said he was going north for some canoeing, after leaving Pepe with whom he had been staying. I found myself envying Steve his freedom after his successful climb. How nice it would be to go travelling again and explore the rest of Patagonia. As Steve wished us luck and left I felt the urge to go with him. It was the first clear sign of faltering interest in what we were doing. I knew I needed to reach the summit soon, before my mind disengaged and moved me on to another project. I wondered if the others were starting to feel the same way.

Hanneke accompanied Steve a short distance down the trail

and then stood for a while in the clearing next to the camp, staring up towards the Towers. I walked across to join her. Silently we gazed up the valley at the threatening black clouds that swirled around the peaks above. The wind was warmer than during the last storm; the air no longer felt bitter. It was exhilarating, and we played balancing games, first leaning into it, and then going limp and allowing it to blow us backwards. Hanneke suddenly looked more serious.

'Do you think they will be having a hard time?'

'Sure to be. They should be back down by now,' I said solemnly, wondering what on earth Paul and Noel were doing. 'Steve's a nice bloke,' I said, changing the subject.

Hanneke's face lit up again. 'Yes, he is. Very kind and so generous. He paid for us to stay in a fantastic hotel in Puerto Natales. I'm going with him on his canoeing trip. It sounds wonderful, paddling around deserted fiords during the day, camping on the beach at night.'

'Have you got room for another?' I half joked. 'And what will you do after that?'

'We thought we might do some travelling in the north of Chile, Steve has suggested that I go and stay with him on his houseboat in San Francisco. I'd planned to go to the States anyway, so I might as well give it a go. I've nothing to lose.'

'Sounds great to me,' I agreed. 'A tour of South America and a free doss in San Francisco – you've certainly landed on your feet.'

'Guess I have,' Hanneke said with a smile. 'Well, it beats going back to England.'

*

In the hut that evening Sean and I were growing anxious. The weather had deteriorated through the afternoon. There was no sign of Paul or Noel, who must have been spending another night sitting out the storm. In a way it made sense, for they wouldn't want to come down having done no climbing at all. We had just finished convincing one another that we were not going to see them that night when we heard crashing sounds in the lean-to. Seconds later Noel walked in.

'Ah, good evening everyone. Is the kettle on?'

'On the way,' Sean spluttered, jumping up and reaching for the pan.

Paul appeared at the door with unruly tufts of matted hair sticking out from his head. There were holes in the knees and elbows of his climbing clothes, which were held together with strips of sticky tape. Both looked as if they had been sleeping rough for weeks. For a few moments there was an uneasy silence, as if two groups of people with nothing in common had just been introduced to each other.

'Is it getting a bit wild up there?' I asked feebly.

A look of concentration spread over Paul's face, as if he were finding the question somewhat demanding.

'Sort of . . .' He paused, nodding his head rhythmically before continuing – 'In fact it's awful up there now. That's why we've come down. We climbed another couple of rope lengths today though . . .'

'Yeah,' Noel interrupted, 'we're getting high up there now. Last night the wind kept lifting the portaledge until the bloody thing was practically airborne.'

'Didn't the wind make it difficult to climb?' I asked.

'No, not too difficult. It's like a deep corner where we are at the moment, so it's quite sheltered.' Paul replied.

With the prevailing winds coming from the west, we were lucky to be on the east side of the mountain. We had not even considered the wind in our choice of objective during the run up to the expedition.

'Listen!' enthused Noel. 'Paul and I have been thinking . . .'

'Sounds dangerous,' I said.

'Well, we couldn't sleep last night. Anyway, we reckon with the climbing we've done today we should be able to go for the summit when next we go up. It's not so far to easy ground, then we'll be able to blast up that to the top.'

'Don't be daft, Noel. All mountains are foreshortened when you look at them from below. From what I've seen, the broken ground will be quite tricky. I can't see us blasting our way up anything.'

'Hey, come on. Where's that positive attitude you're always going on about,' Noel complained. 'If we start thinking it's too difficult, we'll never get up it.'

'It's much farther to the top than you seem to think,' Sean said in support of my caution.

'Well, we've got to go for it some time,' Noel pleaded.

Paul added weight to Noel's argument. 'Look, wait a minute. If Noel has to head back home in five days' time, it's only fair to give him a chance of reaching the top.'

The hut fell silent. We had all put a lot into the climb, but only Noel had fixed work commitments at home and a date by which he would definitely have to leave. Sean looked at me.

'What do you think?'

'I can see their point, but it's no good rushing into trouble just because Noel's got to go home.'

'Right then. How will we go about it?' Sean asked.

'We've got a plan,' Noel announced, still undaunted. 'We reckon that big snow-covered ledge is not far above the top of the fixed ropes. If you guys could fix ropes all the way up to the ledge in a day and then spend a night there, we could come up and join you, and then we'll all go for the top. We might even make it that day. What do you think?'

'Sounds okay to me,' said Sean doubtfully. 'But you'd better bring some bivvy gear as well, in case we don't get to the top that day.'

Paul and Noel nodded and turned their gaze on me.

'What do you think, Simes?' Paul asked.

'I'm happy, so long as you bring the gear in case we all get stuck.'

'Great!' exclaimed Noel, glancing towards the fire. 'How's that brew coming along, Sean?'

Later, I lay awake in my tent. We had come a long way since our first tentative beginnings on the face. Our lack of knowledge and poor preparation in those early stages now seemed embarrassing, although I never thought that the challenge we had set ourselves was going to be easy. But we had stuck with it, even when progress had been slow, and learnt from our mistakes. Now suddenly, reaching the top seemed a real possibility and, against all my superstitions and fears of disappointment, I allowed myself to feel excited by the prospect.

In the morning the weather was still bad and we slipped back into our old routine, all gathering in the hut for a prolonged breakfast. Apart from the cooking, washing up and a brief expedition to collect firewood, very little needed to be done. Paul spent the afternoon ten feet off the ground, wedged in the fork of a tree trunk. When I asked him what he was doing, he looked puzzled, as if it should have been obvious.

'I'm reading,' he said rather irritably, pulling a rolled-up paperback from the pocket of his coat.

The next day the sun shone again. I hurriedly got up, feeling that at last our chance had arrived. Although early, clouds of smoke floated gently up from the hut chimney. Inside, all except Sean were already up. Noel handed me a cup of coffee. There was an air of excitement.

'A beautiful day, eh Simes?' Paul noted, a ridiculous grin filling his face.'

'Yes, wouldn't you know it,' I said sarcastically. 'Just as I was beginning to enjoy lying around in a wet sleeping bag listening to the rain, something was bound to come along to spoil it.'

'Don't worry,' said Noel. 'I promise we'll find somewhere wetter next time we go climbing together.'

'I might just give it a miss. You can have too much of a good thing.'

Despite appearing otherwise, I felt a shiver of apprehension. What lay above the top of our fixed rope? It would be a serious matter if we were forced to retreat hurriedly from high on the mountain. Either Noel had not considered the possibility, or it didn't worry him. His cavalier attitude made it hard to tell. Paul kept an air of calmer confidence about him, but together they had a seemingly unstoppable drive. It was that drive – coupled with Noel's imminent departure – that was now controlling the timetable of events.

Some time later, Sean strolled into the hut, showing little sign of excitement, and made straight for the fire. It never ceased to amaze me how Sean could continue to climb while appearing to have little interest in it or enthusiasm for what he was doing. His attitude seemed at odds with the time and commitment I knew he had put into mountaineering. At times I almost felt embarrassed discussing climbing with him.

'Today's the day, eh Sean?' I said.

'Yep,' he replied through a mouthful of oatcake. 'We'd better sort out some food to take.'

'I thought three days should do us.'

'Better make it four.'

'What time do you think we should go?'

'There's no way we could walk up, jumar to the top of the ropes and still have time to do any climbing. So we might as well have an early evening meal here and head up to the portaledges after that.'

'Oh good,' I said morosely. 'Another whole day to doss around here.'

During the day I finished a few letters, ate an enormous lunch and packed my rucsac. Several attempts at reading had to be abandoned. I found it impossible to concentrate, preferring to lie motionless in my tent, staring at the roof. However I tried, I could not take my mind off our line of ropes stretching up the face, or the anchors to which they were attached. While we had taken every care to secure the ropes properly – most were fastened to several pieces of gear – it was not always easy to gauge how safe they were. I knew from previous experience how crucial anchors could be.

Several years before I had met up with my friend Tommy Curtis in Chamonix at the end of August, and after a few alcoholic days stuck in the town in bad weather, we decided to try the MacIntyre Colton route – a difficult modern climb on the Grandes Jorasses, one of the most impressive peaks in the Mont Blanc range. By lunchtime on the day after leaving the town we stood on the bergschrund at the base of the route. Above us a cone-shaped icefield led up into a deep recess. Three shallow gullies lined with thin, intermittent ribands of ice snaked their way up the very steep ground above the recess. Our chosen route followed the middle streak of ice.

We made easy work of the icefield, climbing unroped up to the start of our chosen gully. There we paused to get the ropes and equipment from our rucsacs. The ground above looked far too steep and difficult to carry on without them. Our decision to put on the ropes was soon vindicated when Tommy took a short fall while entering the gully. It was easy to see the problem when I followed the pitch. Some of the shattered rock was, as we had hoped, covered in a thick coating of ice, allowing progress to be made with ice-axes and crampons. However, in places the coating of ice was thin, and either it had to be painstakingly scraped away so that we could use the handholds on the rock, or alternatively we had to move up using very insecure axe placements. Tommy had fallen when one of these placements ripped out.

The climbing above continued to be difficult, but we made slow steady progress. By the evening we had completed the first hard section of the route and emerged from the shallow gully on to a small icefield. Unable to find a ledge, we chipped a shelf into the ice, placed some ice-screws around it, and settled down for the night, sitting in our sleeping bags and cocooned in a web of rope tied to the ice-screws to prevent us from falling from the shelf.

It was a relief when the dawn finally arrived and we were able to escape the cramped bivouac and get some warmth into our chilled bodies. I led off up the icefield, and as it was easy-angled, I waved for Tommy to stop belaying and follow me. Soon we were moving together – a system commonly used in the mountains on easy ground, for it's quicker than climbing pitch by pitch. We remained roped together and for a couple of hundred feet climbed without any protection, confident that neither of us would fall and pull the other off.

Towards the top of the icefield it became obvious that we would need to pitch the steep wall above. I placed a poor ice-screw, clipped the rope to it and moved up to the base of the wall to look for a belay. The rock was not good – shattered and loose – but I managed to slide a nut in between two wobbly blocks. Tommy continued to move up towards me. The nut alone was far from adequate, but I slipped a small hook attached to my harness through it to allow me to stand in balance while I constructed a decent belay. Then the unexpected happened.

A panic-stricken cry of 'Siiiimoooon!' came up from below. I looked down immediately and, to my horror, saw Tommy cartwheeling down the icefield below. As I had not yet set up the belay I was not holding the rope. I had not even taken in the slack. All I could do was to watch helplessly as Tommy accelerated away from me, taking the slack in the rope with him. My attention then flashed to the nut. Soon the rope would come tight and the full force of the fall would come on to it. I felt sure the nut would be pulled out – and me with it. Then both of us would fall with even greater force on to the single poor ice-screw. If that ripped, we would go all the way to the glacier a thousand feet below.

I had barely considered the consequences of what was going to happen when the rope snatched tight at my waist, pulling me off my feet. Amazingly, both the hook and the nut held.

'My crampon fell off,' Tommy shouted up, lying on his side a hundred and fifty feet below while trying to get it back on his boot again.

Two years before, climbing a different route on the same mountain, I had watched two Japanese climbers fall to their deaths from near the summit when their belay anchor failed to hold. Yet an anchor that I knew was poor had held Tommy's hundred-foot fall, and we were able to continue with our climb.

*

Time passed slowly in the afternoon. Once or twice I left my tent and strutted nervously around the camp, and it was a relief when Noel called from the hut to say the evening meal was ready.

The enormous feast of refried beans, chapattis and grated cheese was a struggle to eat, coming so soon after lunch. I forced the food down, wondering how I was going to walk up the steep path to the Towers, let alone haul myself up the fixed ropes to the portaledge camp, on such an overblown stomach.

The meal passed quietly in an atmosphere of tension which gradually increased the longer it went on. Coffee followed the food, offering a further excuse to delay our departure. At the end of his second cup Sean snapped –

'Right, then. I'm off. See you guys the day after tomorrow.' He put down his mug on the table with a thud and hauled on his rucsac.

'Yeah, see you then.' There was a look of sadness on both Paul's and Noel's faces, as if they were never going to see him again.

'Good luck,' Hanneke said when Sean sauntered out of the door as though he was going no further than down to the pub.

I gave Sean a good head start before saying my own goodbyes, shouting 'Don't be late!' as I left the camp.

It felt good to be on the move again. The tension and air of expectation in the camp had become almost unbearable. I was glad not to have to spend another day there. I almost expected the others to follow me up the path, unable to wait their turn any longer.

I caught up with Sean in the small valley at the side of Laguna Torres and walked silently past him. There was no hurry. It was early evening, and all we needed to do at the portaledge camp was to sleep. Further up, above the lake, the views opened out and I kept stopping to look. The weather had remained perfect all day, the sky completely free of cloud. Now even the daytime breeze had dropped, allowing a blurred reflection of the North Tower to form on the surface of the grey cloudy water of Laguna Torres below. Filled with sediment from the glacier, and surrounded by slopes of boulderous moraine, it looked like an unfinished reservoir, still awaiting the arrival of the landscapers.

As I walked easily up the slushy snow of the Torres Glacier – now stripped down to bare ice in places – I had to weave my way through a labyrinth of crevasses that had been exposed by melting snow. I remembered how, just a few weeks earlier, the glacier had been a uniform white slope and I'd had to plough through thigh-deep snow to get up and across it.

Climbing the ropes up the lower slabs was now easy as the ropes dangled across bare rock. The character of the whole mountain was changing. The conditions were now much better for climbing, and I laughed to myself at how we had struggled to climb such easy terrain. I had no doubt that if we were just starting the climb, it would take only a couple of days to reach the portaledges instead of the nine agonising days it had in fact cost us to set them up.

I reached the portaledge camp in record time. The place was beginning to look well used, with a much larger multi-coloured mosaic of drinks, food and urine staining the snow.

'This place is becoming a shithole,' Sean muttered when he arrived.

'You're not wrong there,' I agreed, pointing to the dwindling snow patch. 'Looks as if we could run out of water soon.'

'Well, let's hope we get this over before that happens.'

The evening was perfect – warm enough to stand comfortably on the ledge, waiting for the final brew to boil. We stood in silence, staring out at the beautiful panorama below, the stillness disturbed by no more than the hum of the stove. It was only when the water boiled over that we snapped out of our trance. I made the drinks and handed one to Sean.

'What time do you want to get going tomorrow?' I asked.

'Can't be too early for me. It'll be a long day.'

'Well, as the fixed ropes now go higher it'll take us a bit longer than before, so shall we say five?'

'Sounds about right,' said Sean with a grin. 'We must be getting keen in our old age.'

SEVEN

Heading for a Fall

It was a relief when the alarm went off the next morning. I had slept little. Anxious and excited about what was to come, I had lain awake for hours, listening to the tossing and turning in Sean's portaledge. The weather had held, and now I felt none of the inertia that had delayed our departure on previous days at the portaledge camp. There was a powerful incentive to get going. If we didn't reach the snow-covered ledge high on the face by evening, we might have to face an uncomfortably exposed bivouac.

Within minutes we were both dressed and packing our rucsacs. Once a lukewarm drink was inside me, I shouldered my rucsac and set off up the fixed rope, leaving Sean to follow behind.

Swinging into space above the camp no longer bothered me and I barely paused between completing the manoeuvre and continuing up the rope. Before long my mind began racing, taking my attention off the climbing. I began to worry about what lay ahead. I knew there were precious few ledges big enough to stand on, let alone lie on. What if the weather broke? There were no certainties. I found myself rehearsing hypo-thetical scenarios, over and over in my mind.

Halfway up the second rope my concerns momentarily shifted as I approached a worn section of rope. I had spotted some signs of wear when we had last come down, but this was much worse. The outer grey sheath had completely worn away, exposing the bundle of white fibres in the core of the rope. I peered at the white section of rope ten feet above me with an intense, morbid curiosity. My weight had flattened it over a sharp edge of rock. I imagined it gradually sawing through each time I moved upwards and expected it to part suddenly, starting a long and violent fall to the glacier over a thousand feet below. When finally I reached the worn stretch, it was nowhere near as bad as I had thought. I laughed nervously at my fears, but I didn't relax again until the jumars supporting my weight were above the fraying section of rope.

Higher up, I passed several more patches of worn rope, some wrapped in adhesive tape that Paul and Noel must have applied to protect them. Passing these points was even more worrying as it was impossible to see the extent of the damage hidden by the tape, even though I felt sure the others would not have covered up any serious fraying.

The higher I went, the better the condition of the rope became. Having been fixed in place more recently, it had had less time to abrade. Above the Scoop, the rope was sound, and I was able to build up a rhythm, but the whole process of climbing the ropes was becoming monotonous.

After four hours of climbing I reached the top and settled down to wait for Sean. The ropes ended halfway up a long corner which continued up to a group of overhangs. There was no obvious way through them. Although the others had climbed only three hundred feet higher, we suddenly seemed to be much further up. I began to think the summit was close. I had noticed before that near the top of a mountain the proportions became smaller, making progress seem greater.

As soon as Sean arrived I set off up the corner. For once, the climbing was straightforward, following an inch-wide crack. I leap-frogged from one Friend to another, only pausing to place the occasional nut in the crack so that I could clip on the rope to protect me in the unlikely event of a fall. Near the top of the corner the crack contained ice, which had to be cleared out with the pick of an ice-axe to allow me to place the Friends. Finally the crack narrowed to a hairline just beneath the overhangs, and I heard Sean shouting up to tell me that I had reached the end of the rope. I pounded a couple of metal pegs into the crack, fastened the ropes to them and yelled down to Sean to come on up.

I felt pleased. We were moving well, even with the hindrance of overloaded rucsacs on our backs. But with all the surplus climbing gear having now been used to fix ropes in place, we no longer needed to pull the black haul-bag up behind us. When Sean arrived, we completed the changeover and he moved up towards the band of overhangs. The climbing was obviously much more difficult. He moved very slowly and deliberately, taking a long time over placing pieces of gear before stopping at the overhang.

'Where to now?'

'Up to the left. Towards that chimney.' I tried to sound reassuring while silently glad that I didn't have to lead the pitch.

Sean found a placement for a peg far to his left and at full stretch tapped it in with his hammer before moving across on to it. Even now the difficult section was far from over, and he continued to move with torturous slowness. Time was being eaten away. Each anxious glance at my watch, revealed the passing of another fifteen minutes of precious daylight.

Eventually Sean reached the chimney and could make faster progress. Higher up, it constricted and formed a bulge. I watched anxiously while he squirmed higher, his entire body wedged inside the fissure. Shouting a torrent of abuse, he inched his way up, forced outwards by the bulge. Suddenly he appeared to be struggling. He reached up above the bulge to place a nut while trying to stop himself sliding back down the chimney by pedalling his right leg furiously on the wall outside the fissure. The nut in place, he paused for a brief rest before lurching upwards and around the bulge, on to the nut he had fought so hard to place. As he stood upright, I looked away in silent relief.

Immediately the rope went tight, tugging at my waist, and a strange metallic clattering sound came from above. I jerked my head upwards, just in time to catch a view of Sean falling through the air beneath the chimney. He bounced once over the line of overhangs and came to a violent halt just below them, forty feet beneath his high point.

'Fuck!' The scream echoed around us as Sean hung in space above, a look of complete dejection on his face.

'Are you all right?' I enquired timidly.

'Yes, yes,' he snapped.

I gazed down at the glacier far below. Sean uttered another stream of curses, and when I looked up again, he was already fixing his jumars to the rope and preparing to climb up once more.

'Sorry. The nut ripped out.'

'So I noticed,' I replied, puzzled by Sean's apology. Any of us could have made a mistake placing a nut in such a difficult position, and it was he who had fallen after all.

I tied his rope to the belay so that he could jumar up it and he quickly reached the top piece of equipment that had arrested his fall. Then I untied the rope from the belay, allowing him to climb above his high point again. After a few upward movements, he paused and looked down.

'How are we doing for time?'

'Not too well. We'll need to find that ledge soon.'

The fall seemed to have calmed Sean. He climbed the chimney without any of the earlier clumsiness and disappeared over the bulge.

'What's it like up there?' I shouted.

There was no reply, but the rope continued to pass slowly through my hands, indicating that the climbing was not getting any easier. I looked at my watch – only two hours of daylight remained. Our chances of finding the ledge we had seen from the glacier below were ebbing away. I started to think about a forced bivouac. Vivid images of the pair of us tied to the rockface in a cocoon of rope filled my mind. The rope started moving faster and the images immediately changed. Now I was imagining Sean scrambling up easy ground to a large snow-covered ledge. Then, just as suddenly as it had started, the rope returned to inching through my hands.

'What's happening?' I yelled.

'There's sod all up here . . .' wafted down from the unseen figure above.

'What about higher up?'

'I don't know.'

I wanted to be up at the top of the rope with Sean, suspiciously imagining that he had overlooked a ledge large enough for us both to spend the night. After another long wait the rope ran out, and Sean called down that he was arranging a belay. The light was already beginning to fade.

I jumared up the rope as quickly as possible, but I lost more precious time passing a knot joining two sections of rope together. It was necessary to secure it to the rock to make abseiling easier. Above the knot the rope was much thinner, as all our thick rope had been used up. It stretched alarmingly as I climbed, and all my fears about the rope breaking returned. Towards the top of the chimney the climbing became awkward, even with the aid of the rope from above. It was easy to understand the problems Sean must have had while leading. Once above the bulge, the angle eased off. The rock held patches of snow and ice and formed a shallow gully up to a small ledge where Sean was standing. I raced up the final section of rope and collapsed in a fit of panting just beneath him.

'It doesn't look good, does it?'

I peered around, convinced that I'd find a large ledge Sean had failed to see.

'Well, that great big ledge we saw has got to be round here somewhere.' I was determined not to let Sean's pessimism go unchallenged. But he was right – it did not look good. Even with some digging, the biggest ledges would offer little more than standing room. It was now nearly dark.

'Pass me the kit. I'm going to take a look up there.' I pointed to a wide crack that led off to the left.

I set off with the equipment dangling loosely around my neck – there was no time to sort it out. It felt strange to be climbing free again and I needed to move quickly into the crack. It was steep at first and required a few strenuous moves, before curving to the left round a corner. As I edged round, the angle eased further and led up to a small snow-covered ledge. Beyond a shallow rib of rock, the terrain looked even more promising.

'Looks good up here,' I shouted, moving up the final section of the crack.

As I grabbed the ledge, something caught my eye deep down inside the crack. I looked again. It was a rope, a piece of old woven nylon rope. Here was the first sign of others since we left the Spanish highpoint at the portaledge camp. Such an old piece of rope could only have come from somewhere near the top. The east face of the mountain had first been climbed some years before climbers stopped using the sort of rope I was looking at. It was a very reassuring indication that we were near to the summit, and the knowledge that others had passed nearby, however long ago, gave me a feeling of confidence.

The angle was now much gentler. A shelf, banked out in snow veered to the left above more steep rock. I sensed that the large ledge was not far away. It *had* to be here.

Following the shelf was easy – a simple matter of kicking steps into the snow. I skirted round the rib of rock and found an open corner filled with a deep cone of snow.

'It's here, Sean,' I shouted into the gloom.

Barely able to control my excitement, I raced up to the top of the snow cone, arranged a belay in the corner and called down for Sean to follow.

I pulled a head torch from the top of my rucsac, turned it on and fixed it to my helmet. The pool of light it created enabled me to examine my surroundings in more detail. The ledge looked quite adequate for our needs. At the very least, it was going to be possible to sit down with our legs outstretched – a true luxury on a mountain face that had provided us with only one other such ledge in the previous three thousand feet of climbing.

I removed my ice-axe from my rucsac and started hacking away at the snow, which was soft, granular and easy to remove. By the time Sean approached I had produced a platform large enough for us both to sit comfortably.

'What do you reckon?' I greeted him, barely able to suppress the satisfaction in my voice.

'Not bad.'

'Not *bad*!' I shrieked. 'It's absolutely brilliant!'

'It'll be all right, I suppose. Once we've made this ledge bigger.'

Sometimes there seemed to be no pleasing him. I worked steadily, enlarging the platform while Sean got the stove going. All that mattered now was making a reasonable place to spend the night. As I dug deeper the snow became more compact and it was necessary to chip out big chunks of ice. Even so, it didn't take long before we were able to put down our mats and get into our sleeping bags. We could even lie down, although our feet hung over the edge of the platform. At last we could relax.

It seemed strange to be in such surroundings after climbing such a long stretch of vertical and overhanging rock. A crack in the rock next to Sean provided the perfect anchor from which to hang the stove, and all around was snow and ice to melt for water. We would only need to move to go to the toilet.

During the day we had both become very dehydrated, carrying only a litre of water each. With Sean taking care of the stove there was little for me to do. I tightened the hood of my sleeping bag and dozed, reappearing with each nudge signalling the arrival of another drink. Sean even melted snow to fill the water bottles for the morning.

When the stove and Sean's headtorch were finally turned off, the darkness and silence felt strange. I opened the hood of my sleeping bag and stared outside. All was calm and still, and the stars shone brightly from an obsidian, moonless sky. The reality of our position started to sink in. It was exciting to think of where we were, how far we had come and the fact that we were so near to the summit. At the same time, I knew we were in a serious and committing position. We were very much alone.

'I hope we reach the top tomorrow,' I said, unable to think of anything else to talk about. There was a long pause before Sean replied.

'Yeah, so do I.'

It was nice to know he was still there.

EIGHT

Storm of Fury

I woke to the familiar sound of fabric flapping in the wind. With it came the dread that the weather had changed, and in our present position that did anything but prompt the lie-in I'd enjoyed at the portaledge camp. If it was necessary to go down, it would have to be done quickly.

I unzipped my bivvy bag, fearing the worst. The sky was overcast and filled with high grey cloud. The granite that had looked warm and golden in the previous day's sun now almost matched the sky in colour and appeared cold. The weather was obviously changing, but was not yet bad enough to stop us climbing.

There was little sign of life from Sean lying cocooned beside me in his sleeping and bivvy bags. I started the stove, deeply aware that somewhere beneath us Noel and Paul would be climbing up the long line of fixed ropes. We needed to start climbing as quickly as possible if we were going to stand any chance of reaching the summit today.

'Hey, Sean, time to get moving.' I gently shook the bundle on the ground next to me and heard a muffled groan. 'Brew's ready and the weather's awful.'

'You're kidding.' The distant croaking voice was followed

by the scream of a zip being yanked open too fast.

'I wish I was. Why don't you come out and see for yourself?'

A blinking head emerged and peered up at the cloud-filled sky.

'Oh, hell! What are we going to do now?'

'Carry on, I guess, and hope for the best. The others will be on their way up by now.'

We didn't linger over breakfast, and by the time we left the warmth of our sleeping bags there was snow in the wind. While we were packing away our equipment the wind dropped and a shroud of mist surrounded us. The stillness scared me, and I felt a tension building in the air, as it does on a humid summer evening when a thunderstorm is forming.

I examined the rock above. It was steep, but at least the way was obvious. Just above the bivouac a small pedestal gave access to a soaring crack that led up to a system of chimneys.

'Do you want me to lead? I asked Sean, knowing that it was his turn, but thinking that it might be quicker if I went first.

'Be my guest.' It was an unhesitating response.

Despite our rush to get started, it was still eight o'clock before I left the ledge. After a few easy moves up on to the pedestal the climbing became hard, the gear placements fiddly and time-consuming. The crack flared into a groove which became deeper and deeper, restricting my movement. Then the groove narrowed, forcing me outwards and making it difficult to place equipment effectively. I remembered the problems Sean had had the day before and hoped I would not make the same mistake.

My limbs seemed on top of each other, always in the wrong place and needing to be pulled free. After rounding a small roof, the crack ran into an open corner and I was able to make faster progress. The mist had cleared and the isolated haven of our overnight ledge could be seen far below. The exposure felt dizzying and unreal. Sean was a tiny figure standing on a small white triangular platform in a sea of rock. A large buttress of rock several hundred feet high in the centre of the glacier appeared little more than a boulder. Down beneath the glacier the muddy green lake, Laguna Torres, looked like a miniature duck pond. I had lost all sense of scale.

The corner was straightforward for a short way and I soon reached a wide crack. I had not expected the need to climb such a feature and quickly checked my remaining equipment, cursing when I found that the largest Friend I had with me was not big enough to fit the crack. In a wave of panic, I thought I would be unable to climb higher.

Feeling lost, I peered down at the ledge, hoping to receive some inspiration or encouragement from Sean. There were now three figures on the ledge. Noel and Paul had joined him.

I looked back at the rock, feeling even more frustrated and guilty for holding them all up. I had to do *something* – and quickly. Then I noticed a faint weakness snaking up the wall about three feet to the right of the crack. It offered the only feasible way higher.

The hairline crack would take only the smallest pieces of equipment, very thin metal pegs, or minute brass nuts. I tapped in a peg, but it would go no more than half an inch into the rock, and I moved up on to it very carefully, half expecting it to pull out. It held, and I placed another peg and moved gingerly up again. After a few moves I began to feel more confident. Just a short distance above, the wide crack narrowed, offering a return to more secure climbing. I just needed to make it to that point.

Every move was precarious. I watched the thin metal pegs flex and twist as I crawled up the vertical rockface, hoping they would hold. The wide crack to my left started to narrow. Just two more moves, I told myself, and then it would be possible to get back to that crack. I made the moves very carefully and felt relieved when I was able to lean to the left and push a Friend into the crack.

I hung on the Friend and looked down at the line of equipment protruding from the otherwise smooth wall, feeling pleased with myself. The worst was over and the way above looked much easier. At last it would be possible to move quickly again, to reach a belay and bring up the others.

I pushed in another Friend and, without even checking the

placement, moved up on to it. Then I removed the one below, knowing that I needed to leave a secure piece of equipment to protect myself and deciding that I could place a good nut just above.

I never got to place the nut. As I stood up level with the Friend I noticed its cams were resting on ice in the crack. I barely had time to feel afraid as the device suddenly ripped from the crack in a shower of ice crystals. It all seemed to happen so slowly. Now you're going to fall, I had time to think before accelerating down into the first of a series of brutal impacts. I saw a bright flash of light, followed by darkness. My limbs flailed, first one way then the other, as I ricocheted down the rock. The downward motion was accompanied by equally violent ones from above as my fall was arrested by piece after piece of equipment ripping from the hairline crack. It seemed as if no part of my body was free from the battering.

Then just as suddenly as it had started, it stopped. A sickening jerk wrenched into my chest and stomach and left me hanging limply on the rope. After a few anxious moments my vision returned and the sight shocked me. I was hanging upright, but facing outwards, just ten feet above the bivouac ledge. I looked down at the others, who were staring at me.

For some time my brain refused to function. I simply hung on the rope in a dream-like state, unable to take in what had happened. It was hard to know who was more shocked, for the others looked equally dazed. They stared at me as if I were some apparition in a freak show. Nobody spoke. I wondered if blood was pouring from my ears, or if one of my limbs was sticking out at an incongruous angle. Perhaps they could see something I couldn't feel. I scanned my body, but it all appeared to be intact. As my feeling slowly returned my left elbow hurt.

'Are you all right?' Sean finally asked.

'I think so.' My voice sounded cracked.

The worry on the faces of the others dissolved, Noel's buckling into a wry smile which he tried to contain.

'What a spectacular lob!' he exclaimed.

Paul began to snigger, first covering his mouth with his

hand and then looking away. Even Sean was smiling now.

'I'm going to have to come down,' I said weakly. 'Can you lower me, Sean?'

Sean let out rope quickly, but nothing happened. I remained where I was.

'The rope's jammed,' he explained. 'You'll have to untie the red rope before I can lower you down.'

I fumbled with the knots at my waist, untying the red rope and then starting on the other.

'Stop!' shouted Noel. 'Don't untie that knot, you'll fall.' The thought that I needed to remain tied to one rope had not even occurred to me.

Through a combination of down-climbing and lowering, I rejoined the others on the ledge. I felt very shaky and stood trembling, looking up to where I had come off. The fall had been a long one, perhaps a hundred feet. I had stopped just short of the pedestal of rock above the ledge. If I had continued falling a few feet more, I would have smashed into the upward pointing fin of rock. No one needed to tell me how lucky I had been.

'I've hurt my arm. I don't think I'll be able to go back up and finish the pitch,' I said rather pathetically.

'Don't worry about that, I'll go,' Noel reassured me. 'What about your arm?'

Everyone now looked very concerned again. I felt my left elbow with my right hand. It was swollen, but the pain was not intense, although that could have been due to a state of shock.

'I don't think it's broken,' I pronounced, not altogether convinced by my diagnosis, but not wanting to make a fuss. A lot of time had been lost by my slow progress above the bivouac ledge and the fall, and Noel was now anxious to leave. Our chance of reaching the summit that day already seemed to have gone. I began to feel cold. As Noel prepared to leave I started to unpack my sleeping bag.

'Don't forget to take the large Friend,' I advised him, having spotted the piece of equipment that would have prevented my fall hanging from the belay next to Sean.

Noel left as I slid inside my sleeping bag. Effectively out of the climbing for the day, I felt the shock begin to dissolve into anger. Why had I rushed such a difficult section of climbing, and why had I not taken the opportunity to place a good piece of protection as soon as I'd regained the wide crack? I hadn't even bothered to take with me a vital piece of equipment. It was so stupid of me! In my rush to save time I had been careless. It had nothing to do with being over confident. I was simply rushing when I should have been careful. Rather than save time, my carelessness had cost us time. I cursed myself. I'd put myself and the others at risk by making such a serious error so high on the mountain, and there was still the possibility that the injury to my arm would force me to go down.

I felt miserable, too engrossed with self-pity to pay any attention to the weather or what the others were doing. When I did start looking round, the sight depressed me still further. The day had deteriorated and we were now in the midst of a storm. The wind was stronger than ever, and it was snowing quite heavily, although none was falling on our sheltered ledge. In fact, the snow was not so much falling as being blown horizontally through the air. The ominous cap of black cloud had returned to the top of the mountain.

'See you later, Simes,' Paul said as he left to join Noel above. I hardly noticed him leave.

As I sat there, staring out into the cloud and snow with my elbow throbbing, what we were doing seemed utterly absurd. It always did at such moments. It was all so unfair. How much more work, effort and suffering was going to be necessary for us to reach the top? Hadn't we done enough already? At the same time I knew I did not want to go down. We had invested far too much to give up now.

Sean soon returned to his sleeping bag and started up the stove again. We sat on the ledge like a couple of down and outs watching the day go by. Up above, Noel and Paul made steady progress, climbing a chimney above the crack from which I had fallen before disappearing from sight round an overhang fringed with enormous icicles. The wind gradually increased, plucking huge chunks of rime from the top of the mountain. The sky above was filled with them, and I tracked the biggest pieces as they spun away eastwards towards the Pampas. Each time we took a piss off the ledge our urine flew vertically upwards, as if gravity had somehow been magically reversed.

Later, after the others had been out of sight for some time, I began to wonder if they had made a dash for the summit without us, but after a short time they reappeared, sliding down the ropes, and we fired up the stove.

Noel arrived first. He looked drawn.

'Is it getting easier up there?' I asked.

'Afraid not. Is that a brew on the way?'

Sean handed Noel a cup of some unidentifiable hot liquid. He looked very cold. Paul was no better. The pair of them simply stood between Sean and me, huddled over their cups as if they expected to gain some miraculous warmth from them. Once their drinks were finished, they too got into their sleeping bags.

With all four of us on the ledge there was not much space. Sitting shoulder to shoulder, with the storm howling around us, we looked a sorry bunch.

I asked Paul the same question as I'd put to Noel. 'Is the climbing getting easier, Paul?'

'Well, sort of,' he replied. I was none the wiser.

'How, exactly?'

'Well, there's this crack going up a steep slab, where we stopped. It looks like it leads up to a snowy gully.'

'Could you see the summit?'

'Not really.'

'Bollocks!' I shouted into the wind. The others stared at me nervously. 'We must be near now, surely.' I felt my voice cracking as I spoke.

It was all getting to be too much, but still no one spoke of going down, although I didn't doubt for one moment that we were all thinking about it. There was little to do but sit and wait to see what the morning would bring.

The wind steadily increased during the evening, as it had

done throughout the day. By nightfall it had risen to a deafening roar. We had all expected the Patagonian weather to be bad – the wind there is notorious – but this was beyond our grimmest expectations. Shortly after dark the strongest gusts of wind started making a noise like an enormous whip being cracked as they blasted round the summit. Then it sounded as if the air was somehow being torn apart. The noises terrified me, I had heard nothing like it before. The continual din, and the fear it brought, prevented much sleep. I managed to doze occasionally, but most of the time I just lay worrying about the day ahead, wishing the storm would stop. At least my arm felt better.

Eventually it started to get light. The dawn was very slow – the thick, dark cover of cloud saw to that – and the wind was no calmer. It was warmer though, and the air felt laden with moisture, hinting that there was still worse to come.

We went through the motions of starting the day, automatically and in almost complete silence. Everyone's drive seemed to have been exhausted. A retreat appeared inevitable, although no one mentioned the subject. It was hurtful even to think of it. We just ate and drank and stared into the greyness, faces furrowed with tiredness and stress.

'We should start down soon,' Sean announced suddenly.

'I want to try for the top,' Noel said quietly.

'It's hopeless, Noel. Heaven knows what the weather is going to throw at us next,' Sean said irritably, looking at Noel as if he had taken leave of his senses.

'But it's my last chance,' Noel pleaded. 'I'll have to leave as soon as we return to base camp. I really have to get back to my work in Oxford.'

Paul seemed strangely undecided. I thought of all our hard work and how close we were to success. More than anything, I thought of going down over three thousand feet of rope only to have to come all the way back up again. The idea appalled me. I'd never felt particularly comfortable climbing up the fixed ropes, and now some of them had been in place for over a month. They were already badly worn in places and the storm in progress would be doing them even more damage. I did not

112

want to climb back up them again. Of that I was sure. Going up was a different matter.

'I'll go with you, Noel,' I said. The words seemed to come from nowhere.

'Great. Let's get going then.' Noel's enthusiasm sprang to life once more.

'We'll follow you up,' Paul said softly.

We packed our things and Noel set off up the rope. The storm continued to howl. Soon it was my turn to follow and I immediately began to wonder if I had made the right decision. Sean and I had had to fix a section of seven-millimetre rope to reach the ledge, but for the rest of the climb the thinnest rope we had used was nine millimetres in diameter. Paul and Noel had fixed more of the thin rope above. It was all we had left. The rope stretched alarmingly when I put my weight on to it. I started jumaring, and with each move the rope bounced, no doubt sawing over on edges of rock in the process. There was precious little of it to be worn away, and I felt sure it would snap.

I looked up at Noel and wondered if he was thinking the same thing, whether dangling on tiny threads of rope day after day, thousands of feet up a sheer mountain face actually bothered him. He did not give the impression that it did.

We gained height steadily. I paused at the spot where I had fallen and shook my head. We might have completed the climb the day before but for my mistake. Now the crack looked so innocuous.

The ropes followed a line of chimneys leading up to the overhang fringed with icicles, which was now pouring with water. Even though it was still snowing, a thaw had set in. Noel disappeared in the waterfall while climbing round the lip of the overhang, dislodging as he went great chunks of ice which flew out past me.

I became very worried approaching the overhang, and not only by the water. The lip formed a very sharp edge and the rope hung right over it. There was little to do but hope. The final ten feet up to the roof were appalling. The rope hung free, straight up through the line of the waterfall which cascaded down over my head. I climbed as quickly as possible, but it was not easy. Water poured down the back of my jacket, spinning me round at the same time. The drenching left me numb.

Above the overhang Noel was waiting on a fairly wide but exposed ledge. A steep icy gully soared above us, and water poured down it. Ropes hung down a rock rib to the left. The sky was darker than ever, and there was no shelter from the relentless wind.

Noel pointed upwards before climbing up the ropes and round the rock rib out of sight. I settled down for what was obviously going to be an uncomfortable spell of belaying.

The wait was terrifying. The wind increased in intensity, making the strangest and most frightening sounds as torrents of water came down from above. A waterfall started to flow down the wall to the right of the ledge and swirled around wildly in the wind. I dreaded the strongest gusts, which vaporised the water and blew it into my face with the force of a high pressure hose. It felt as if I would be blown away at any minute. My position was getting desperate, and I did not doubt that Noel's was even worse.

After what seemed like an eternity the ropes tugged from above. It was the only way Noel could signal for me to follow. I leaped at the chance to leave the ledge and escape the drenching. Although it took a long time to fix my jumars to the rope with numb cold hands, it felt good to be getting some warmth circulating.

Once round the rock rib, the ropes followed a crack diagonally to the left up a steep slab which was awash with running water. Through the mist, snow and water, I could just make out Noel hanging, curled up in the foetal position, at the end of the rope. As I moved up towards him I knew we had reached the end of the line. Retreating was no longer just desirable, it was a matter of survival.

While I climbed higher and removed pieces of equipment that Noel had placed in the crack, a large loop of rope formed beneath me and a long section of crack leading up to Noel became bare of any protection. It became obvious that I would have to take a large pendulum leftwards in order to climb higher. I approached the last piece of gear with absolute fear, unclipped it from the rope while still hanging on to the crack, and then let go. The swing swiftly gathered momentum as I slid across the smooth slab before launching into space over the lip of an overhang. I hung a few feet beneath it, feeling sick. The rock overhung everything down to the slabs at the base of the face. Spinning slowly round, I looked down through my legs and retched. Panic-stricken, I spun back and swarmed up the rope. I finally stopped well above the overhang. Another spurt up the rope took me up to just below Noel.

As I arrived Noel uncurled and sat upright, releasing a bout of uncontrollable shaking. He was soaking, and his eyes were filled with tears.

'I've got to go down,' he said apologetically through chattering teeth.

'I know,' I said, feeling my own eyes watering. 'The sooner the better.'

'Do you mind if I go first?' Noel asked with typical politeness. I shook my head, wondering why he had felt it necessary to ask.

We changed places and Noel slid off down the rope, leaving me alone in the storm. Water was now running everywhere and dancing in the air. Not far above, the rock slab ended in a broad, shallow, snow-lined couloir, capped about fifty feet higher by a small roof. It was hard to see what lay above, but there were no more soaring walls of granite, the ground was much more broken and reasonably angled. I felt cheated; we were obviously not far beneath the summit. We deserved to be up there, and yet we had no choice but to go down. I did not think I would be able to summon the drive to come all the way back up here again.

The rope soon came slack and I started down. I could not remember ever feeling so bad about retreating from a mountain. All that mattered now was getting down.

I took great care on the first abseil, terrified of repeating the swing under the overhang. Several times I slipped on the wet greasy rock, but managed to grab features to regain my balance.

Below the roof the flow of the waterfall had increased dramatically. For a few moments I was engulfed in it and had to hold my breath before emerging from the torrent.

Paul had waited for me at the bivouac ledge. Having seen the state in which Noel had arrived, he wanted to make sure I was all right. The others had left, hoping to escape the worst of the storm further down. Seeing how drenched I was, Paul waved me past. It was now a headlong rush down the ropes and as such it was each for himself.

I slid down the ropes in an almost uncontrollable panic, only pausing at rope change-overs, or to shelter from the most severe gusts of wind. Mercifully, the lower I went, the less water there was running down the mountain.

Beneath the chimney, where Sean had fallen on the way up, the knot joining two ropes was in mid-air. To pass it, I needed to swap the descender to the lower side. I had envisaged the problem on the way up and had secured the knot to a nut placed in the rock nearby, knowing it would make coming down much simpler. The nut now hung mockingly from the rope, removed by the violent whipping of the wind.

Getting round the knot proved an exhausting struggle. I soon got myself tangled in a web of jumars and slings, cursing the fact that I had not made a better job of securing the nut on the way up. As I tried desperately to free myself, there was the constant worry that I was freeing the wrong piece of kit, forcing me to check every decision and movement over and over again.

Lower down, I came out of the shallow corner which had offered a little protection from the wind. Suddenly it was hitting me with full force again, hurling me from side to side. I longed for it to stop, but if anything it grew worse. The section between the bottom of the Coffin and the middle of the Scoop was sickeningly exposed. Here I was completely in the open on a bare granite wall with no features to protect me from the wind.

As I approached the portaledge camp I could see the others and felt increasingly safe, even though I knew it would be impossible to relax completely until we were all back in the base camp. Finally, I plunged down the last section of rope and pulled myself on to the ledge beneath the portaledges. The others were huddled together in the centre of the ledge.

'What are you doing?' I asked Noel.

'Making a brew.'

'Can't that wait?' I spat testily, to be met with a blank expression. The stove was barely working because of the wind.

'Did you see Noel's Karrimat?' Paul asked as he arrived at the ledge.

'What . . . ?'

'Noel's Karrimat. The wind caught it as he was trying to pack it away, up at the bivouac.' Paul was laughing now. 'Blew it straight up into the air past you. We watched it soaring off towards the Pampas.'

'I'll see you later.' My sense of humour had deserted me. 'Good luck with the brew,' I shouted aggressively as I started down the final section to the glacier.

The weather had briefly brightened, but now it was darker than ever. A huge black cloud seemed to be following me down the mountain. Soon the air was alive with hail stones, penetrating every weakness in my clothing and stinging my face. Squinting, with my head down, I continued descending the lower slabs, wondering what the weather could possibly throw at us next.

The hail continued unabated, dislodging the others from the camp above. I watched them hastily abseiling the corner below the portaledges, wondering if they had managed to complete their brew. It seemed unlikely.

Despite the hail, it was easier to get down the lower slabs now that they were almost free of snow and ice. Ropes and equipment abandoned on the previous Spanish attempts were now exposed, making it look like the litter it was. The mess incensed me despite my own plight.

Wearily I made the final abseil, with only just enough rope to swing across a large bergschrund that had opened between the rock and snow slope on the edge of the glacier. Once off the end of the rope, I slumped into the snow, tears of relief rolling down my cheeks.

After retrieving my ice axe from the end of the rope I set off across the glacier. A roar of wind coming from the notch between the Central and South Towers tracked down from above and within seconds the sound was deafening. A wall of air slammed into my chest and my feet lifted from under me. For a moment I was weightless, before landing heavily on my back in the snow.

I scampered across the glacier between the gusts of wind, lying face down with my axe planted in the snow as each gust passed. It was the final straw. I filled with anger at Patagonia and its atrocious weather. I hated myself for coming to such a place. Between gusts in the wind I stood in the centre of the glacier waving my fist at the mountain.

'Baaastaaard!' I shrieked into the storm.

Once across the glacier, the going got easier. The wind was now behind me and blew me downhill. My walk became more of a wind-assisted stagger, but at least it was quick. I fell regularly and heavily but righted myself instantly and carried on downwards.

Inside the forest all was calm. I ran down the twisting path, thankful to be still alive. I could not remember trees and plants ever looking so beautiful.

At the base camp I dumped my rucsac outside my tent and slumped on to it. For a few minutes I just stared up at the sky. Then Hanneke came rushing over from her tent, an eager look on her face.

'Have you done it?' she asked excitedly. I shook my head.

NINE

A Night on the Town

I felt exhausted, defeated both mentally and physically, yet my mind kept on racing dementedly, giving me no rest. I knew that reaching the summit was important to Noel and now, despite his hard work and unflagging enthusiasm, his chance had gone. He would have to return home. But the summit had become important to all of us. On other expeditions, where I had not been involved in fixing ropes, reaching the top had usually been a bonus. There had always been the pleasure of movement and exploration. I had never before focussed myself so singularly on one objective. The only acceptable conclusion to the present venture was to try again to reach the top, and that meant climbing back up those three thousand feet of ropes which in places were now badly worn. The prospect seemed daunting. Perhaps my body would be strong enough, given a couple of days' rest, but would my mind? I doubted it.

I wanted to be somewhere else, not necessarily away from the rugged open beauty of Patagonia, just away from the Central Tower of Paine. I needed to be out of its sphere of influence. It seemed ironic: climbing is often said to be some sort of escape, and here I was wanting to be released from the escape.

Noel arrived back in the camp and immediately started

119

packing his things. Although it was late in the afternoon, he had decided there was no point in delaying his long journey home. In the short time that I had known him, I had never seen him looking so miserable. I went over to help him.

'So, you're off then?' I said solemnly.

'Yes, unfortunately. I can't stay any longer.' His voice was tinged with sadness. 'Besides,' he continued, 'if I get down to the Estancia tonight, I'll be able to catch the bus to Puerto Natales in the morning. The others have been talking about coming along to see me off.'

'Good,' I said. 'We could all do with a break.'

As soon as Paul and Sean arrived, we all gathered together a few belongings. There was no discussion about how long we would spend in town; it seemed unimportant. There was just an overwhelming momentum to leave. A panic had overtaken us. Like refugees escaping from a conquering army, we fled the camp.

I needed space in which to think about what had happened, what to do next, and simply to get away from the others. I left the camp first and raced down the path, pausing briefly to look up at the cauldron of bubbling black clouds hanging over the Towers. It seemed strange to think that just two hours before we had been up there among them, battling for our lives.

In stark contrast to that sterile world, the forest around me radiated life. Beside the path, huge beds of white orchids and yellow violas stretched as far as could be seen. Birds sung in the trees. I walked in a dream, both stunned and moved by the peace and beauty of the place.

Once I felt sure the others would not catch up with me, I allowed myself to stop occasionally and pick flowers. I stared into their delicate, coloured petals and drew heavy breaths of their scent. It felt very good to be alive.

Soon I was out of the forest, twisting down a steep open hillside that led to the Estancia. The land below was rolling, less forested, and dotted with lakes, each with its own distinct colour, ranging from copper sulphate blue to vivid turquoise and chalky grey. I felt some release in the space after the confinement of the steep, tree-lined valley of our base camp and the fear up on the wall.

At the bottom of the hill the path turned sharply on to a wooden footbridge across a river. I skirted round a bluff and the Estancia came into sight. Although the mountains were still stormy, shafts of evening sunlight were falling on to the tall sombre pine trees surrounding the buildings. The frame of a new wooden guest house, which had been no more than foundations when we first arrived, stood out in the open nearby.

I walked past the old stone buildings on to an imposing tree-lined drive, through a gate and out on to open grassland where a rough gravel road led me a short distance to Pepe's hut. A group of people sat outside around a large open fire above which a sheep carcass was strapped to a wooden frame, as if it had been crucified. As I approached Pepe stood up to greet me.

'Hi, man. How's it going.'

'Okay,' I lied, dodging any need to go through the painful details of our failure.

Discarding my rucsac, I joined the group, unable to take my eyes off the roasting meat, the delicious smell of which made my stomach churn. Pepe introduced me to his wife and children, explaining that they were up from Punta Arenas to visit for a few days. His situation did not seem compatible with that of a family man, living as he did in a tiny wooden hut no bigger than a garden shed. I wondered where they were all going to sleep.

'What have you been doing?' I asked.

'Too much work, man,' Pepe replied, to the obvious delight of his wife. 'There're so many tourists this year.'

When the others arrived Pepe invited us to share their barbecue. It was typical of his warmth and hospitality. The evening was wonderful. The wind dropped and the rolling foothills were bathed in a rich golden light. The tall grass shimmered in a light breeze and flocks of geese grazed all around without the slightest shyness, their melancholy calls mixing with our talk and laughter.

Later I lay in my sleeping bag under the star-studded sky, tired to the point of exhaustion but unable to sleep. My mind was still churning, still struggling for survival even though my surroundings no longer required it. And up above me, not far away, were the Towers, the cause of all my anxiety. I felt sure I did not have the will to go back and try again. For the third night in a row I hardly slept.

In the morning Pepe drove us in his jeep two miles down a rough track to the police post on the road at the entrance to the National Park. We were all subdued and sat in silence by the small collection of huts, waiting for the bus.

My disappointment had returned, and I looked up into the clouds shrouding the Towers, wondering what might have been. In such a mood even the beauty of the place held little appeal.

Eventually, a plume of dust appeared at the side of the lake and moved towards us. A few minutes later the bus arrived and we hurried aboard. Inside were a few other tourists, but I managed to get a seat on my own. I felt I had little in common with them, and did not want to join in their lively, excited chatter. They viewed our bedraggled appearance with amazement, no doubt wondering what we had been doing to get in such a state. I had no desire to explain, and fortunately no one asked. I simply stared out of the window, watching the Pampas go flashing by, without really registering what I was seeing. My mind was elsewhere.

The other tourists on the bus all looked happy and contented, excited by exploring new unfamiliar territory and the fresh experiences picked up along the way. Why did we want more? Presumably they had found adventure, or something lacking from their lives at home. Perhaps they were disillusioned with work or some other part of their routine and needed to escape for a time to relax, to think with a clarity not possible while surrounded by the clutter of everyday life. Or maybe they were simply on holiday, having a good time. It was hard to know, but they appeared to have found what they were looking for. Success was still eluding us. I envied the travellers and wished my own needs were simpler.

Suddenly everything seemed confusing. For months the focus of my thoughts had been on climbing the Central Tower of Paine. Now that was on hold, abandoned for the time being. Not to try again would make a mockery of all the time and effort I had already invested. If I was willing to give up now, had I been really committed to the project in the first place? The more I thought about it, the more depressed and confused I became.

The bus skirted another lake, shimmering with heat haze and the radiant pinks of a large flock of flamingos. By now I was conducting a witch hunt through my own mind, trying desperately to answer questions which over and over again I had already dismissed as unanswerable. Why had I lost the will to get to the summit? What had become of the stamina I once enjoyed and could rely upon? After a climbing trip last summer I had returned home physically exhausted and before long had slumped into a state of deep depression. For days I was confined to bed, fearful of going completely mad. What had become of me? After years of carefree travelling why did I so desperately want to change?

What had appeared, just a few years before, to be an ideal way to live, suddenly seemed totally undesirable. I was tiring of my itinerant ways, of continually moving, carrying all my belongings around in a rucsac like a perpetual hitch-hiker. I began to consider my own mortality, and started to think I might have to make some provision for when I was older. It had all happened so suddenly and unexpectedly that it came as a shocking revelation, making me feel very insecure and vulnerable. Before there was time to act, however, I found myself coming to Chile. Our failure to climb the mountain had brought my own problems to crisis point again.

In the seat behind me Noel was having his own crisis and pouring his heart out to Paul.

'I can't go back now. Now when we're so close to success,' he said, his voice quivering as if he were going to burst into tears.

'Maybe you should stay for just a few more days,' Paul suggested sympathetically.

'But I have to get back to Oxford,' Noel spluttered, clutching his forehead.

I felt sorry for Noel, but I was quite unable to offer any advice while smothered in my own turmoil. Farther down the bus Sean too was staring blankly out of the window, seemingly oblivious of what was happening around him. He looked devastated. In fact the three of us must have appeared to be embarking on a collective breakdown. Only Paul remained in a positive frame of mind.

As we approached Puerto Natales the flat Pampas gave way to rolling, cultivated countryside, with neat white wooden houses dotted about between fields of sheep. It was a relief when the bus finally cleared the crest of a hill, revealing the large sea inlet with Puerto Natales at its head, gathered speed down the hill, joined a tarmac road and drove into the centre of the small town.

We staggered from the bus and made our way down the plain well-kept streets into a residential area where many of the small wooden bungalows had 'hosteria' signs above their front doors. We booked ourselves into one, stashed away our gear and walked to the sea front where we found the restaurant we had discovered on our first visit to the town. Despite our dishevelled appearance, the proprietor recognised us at once and welcomed us as if we were long-standing customers.

We drank a round of beers before sitting down at a table, and then ordered another. Only when seated, with the beer rushing to my head, did I begin to relax. After four days of frantic activity and minimal sleep, we could finally take it easy. Smiles returned to our faces. We could laugh at ourselves again, at each other and at what had happened in the previous days. Soon we were laughing at every feeble joke, at the antics of other customers and at the staff. Now everything was hilarious. The world was wonderful again. I began to think that maybe our time up on the mountain had not been so bad after all.

The food came, course after course, with waiters continually taking orders, bringing and removing dishes. Huge avocado salads and salmon steaks, dwarfing the plates on which they sat, along with baskets of chips were consumed in minutes. We ordered again – there seemed no end to our appetites. The table disappeared from view under empty beer bottles.

Gradually the pace of our eating and drinking slowed, finally stalling with double helpings of sweets and liqueurs. At eight in the evening we decided to leave – we had been in the restaurant over seven hours. Even the shock of the bill did little to dampen our celebrations. We happily handed over most of our remaining money.

There was no suggestion of an early night as we weaved our way back into the centre of town in search of a lively bar. Being Friday, the smartly dressed young people of Puerto Natales were out in numbers. A large group of them huddled together outside a bar in the main square. We made our way inside.

The bar was large, with hardly any spare seats around the rows of tables. We found some space in a corner and ordered more beer. After weeks of solitude, I found it strange being surrounded by so many people, and felt content just to observe from a distance. I began to feel very drowsy.

Paul and Sean plunged into discussion with a group on the next table, leaving Noel and I to sit it out quietly. Later Paul came over, full of excitement.

'Those guys I've been talking to say everyone goes to the Miladon Disco on Friday night. Apparently people even come over from Argentina for it. What do you think?'

'Oh, no. I need some sleep,' Noel said with a stifled yawn. 'I think I'll go back to the hosteria.'

Paul looked eagerly towards me. 'What about you, Simes?'

'I think I'll go with Noel,' I said reluctantly, already feeling a little melancholy and worried about the effect of more beer.

'Oh, come on,' Paul pleaded. I shook my head.

Sean looked even more disappointed when we got up to leave. He tried again to persuade us to stay, but our minds were made up. We said goodnight and left.

*

It was blissful to lie on a real bed for the first time in over a month. I pulled the clean sheets over my body and my accumulated aches and stiffness dissolved. Within moments I was asleep.

125

I awoke slowly and reluctantly to the accompaniment of strange sounds. It felt very early. I peered round the room, trying to discover where the noise could be coming from and who to blame for interrupting my much needed sleep. Noel was awake now, and we looked at each other across the room. The other two beds were empty. Eventually I located the sound. Someone was tapping on the window.

I pulled back the curtains, squinting into the early morning sun. Paul was standing outside. I opened the window.

'What the fuck are you playing at?' I shouted at him, with more irritation than I felt.

For a moment Paul just stared at me, puzzled by my hostility. I soon realised that he was exceedingly drunk. His entire body was swaying from side to side in an elastic, rhythmic motion, as if he were made entirely of rubber. His feet miraculously stayed put, as if they were nailed to the ground. He reeked of alcohol.

'I've loshSean,' he exclaimed, slurring the two 's'es together.

Noel came to the window, laughing at the vision outside. I went to the front door, opened it, and dragged Paul into our room, where he collapsed on to a bed.

'I've lost Sean.' Paul repeated again and again.

'Shhh!' I hissed at him. 'You'll wake everyone up.'

Paul took no notice and went on repeating his statement, each time in a louder and more hysterical voice.

'I think he's lost Sean,' Noel quipped.

'Where have you lost him?' I asked.

'I don't know,' came the unhelpful answer.

I tried a different tack. 'Is he hurt or in trouble?'

'No, I don't think ssho . . .'

'Maybe we should go and look for him,' suggested Noel.

'Where?' I demanded angrily. 'Besides, he's big enough and daft enough to look after himself.'

Paul started ranting again, becoming more and more agitated. Then he burst into tears.

'Where did you last see him?' I persisted.

'I don't know.' He sobbed. 'We went to the Miladon, and

then some other place. Sean got really plastered.' Paul started giggling. 'Then he drank a bottle of pisco and they threw us out. Sean fell over and wouldn't get up. I tried to lift him, but he just didn't move.' Paul began sobbing again.

'Where was this?' Noel asked.

'I dunno . . .'

'Why don't you get some sleep, Paul?' I suggested, trying to take off his shoes.

'But we got to find him,' Paul said loudly as he struggled away from me.

'We'll go and look for Sean. You stay here and get some rest.'

'No. I'll go with you.'

No amount of persuading could get Paul to change his mind. Between us Noel and I stood him up and reluctantly dragged him out into the street.

It was a brilliant sunny morning, but as it was not yet seven o'clock, the streets were deserted. The tiresome prospect of looking for Sean made me feel resentful. Paul was barely able to stand.

We wandered slowly from street to street until we reached the part of town where Paul thought he had last seen Sean, but he was unable to remember exactly where they had been. The streets were arranged in blocks, one looking very much like another, with small trees planted in the verges in front of rows of neat wooden bungalows. Paul could not distinguish one from another, and I was starting to lose my patience.

'I've just remembered. It wasn't a club, more of a private house really,' he announced suddenly, then adding thoughtfully, 'I think it might have been a brothel.'

The idea of Paul and Sean in a brothel sent Noel and I into gusts of raucous laughter. It was not a place I could imagine either of them visiting.

'It was the only place still open,' Paul explained.

As we turned a corner, already searching streets we had been along before, we spotted a couple of policemen. They looked mean in their black uniforms and knee-length leather boots. I couldn't imagine them responding kindly to drunks littering the pavements of their smart little town.

'Maybe the police have taken him away,' I suggested.

'Yeah. Maybe he spent the night in a cold prison cell,' Noel said with relish. It certainly seemed the most likely explanation as Paul was adamant that we were looking in the right part of town.

'It's over here.' Paul had stopped and was pointing to a quiet domestic house we had walked past at least half a dozen times before. It seemed unlikely.

'This is it,' he insisted. 'I recognise the door.'

There was no sign of Sean, and the door was locked, but there was a vomit stain on the pavement outside.

'I think the police have taken him in,' I repeated. 'If he doesn't turn up in the next couple of hours, I'll go down to the station and see if I can find him.'

I felt angry that we had wasted so much time looking for him, but at the same time was worried. We sauntered slowly back to the hosteria. At least the walk had sobered Paul up a bit.

'I don't know about you, but I'm ready for some breakfast,' I said to Noel as we made our way back inside.

A pot of coffee sat on the stove in the kitchen and our hosts, a kindly old couple, motioned me to a seat at the table in the centre of the room. Paul crashed clumsily on to a chair. I desperately hoped he wouldn't do anything embarrassing. Noel came in and waved to me.

'Come and look at this.'

I followed him to the bedroom. Sean was asleep on the bed nearest to the door. He was lying half naked, sprawled out diagonally across the bed, clutching a blanket covered in vomit. Noel sniggered and I couldn't help a smile crossing my face despite still feeling angry. There seemed no point in waking him.

Paul was already tucking into breadcakes and jam when we returned to the kitchen. The woman handed Noel and I each a cup of coffee.

'I've been thinking,' said Noel. 'I'm going to be late whatever happens. I should be in Oxford now, so I might as well come back to the mountain with you. But if for any reason we can't go straight up on to the face, I'll leave.'

'Good one,' said Paul loudly, obviously pleased by Noel's decision.

I didn't know what to think. Of course it would be good for Noel to have the chance of another go at the summit, but it was a very slim chance. I had the feeling, from the way he spoke, that he had allowed himself a small compromise but was already thinking more about his work in Oxford than the climb.

'What will you do?' Noel asked me.

'I don't know. When we were up at the top of the ropes together and realised it was hopeless, I told myself there was no way I was going back up there again. Now – I'm not sure. Either way, I'm going to stay to the end.'

After breakfast I headed into town on my own and wandered aimlessly through the streets, allowing myself coffee in a café and bars of chocolate. The town had an air of sadness about it, as if it had been set up to become a bustling regional capital and it had never really happened. I walked down to the sea front. Black swans paddled slowly around in the clear still sea water. A group of penguins were fishing from the small pier. In such a peaceful place, the thought of returning to the mountains didn't seem so bad, although my fears about climbing could not be banished entirely.

By the time I returned to the hosteria, Sean was awake and trying to clean himself up.

'What happened to you?' I asked sternly. 'Paul was beside himself when he turned up here this morning. We spent hours looking for you. We thought the police had picked you up.'

Sean looked surprised at all the fuss I was making.

'Oh, someone took pity on me and pulled me inside his house. I slept on the floor for a while before coming back here.'

At any other time I would have found Sean's story funny, but in my present state I was unable to laugh. More than anything I felt peevishly annoyed and wanted him to know it.

'Some night out, eh?' Sean quipped with a nervous giggle.

'I'll see you later,' I said, and left.

I was some way up the street before I calmed down. I could not understand why Sean's behaviour bothered me so much. Why was I so up tight? I was usually quite passive on climbing trips and rarely got angry with others, or was phased by a run of bad luck. Sure, I had had disappointments, even depression, but never this all-consuming internal rage.

Then, all at once, I realised what it all meant. People had often said to me, 'You just don't care what happens', or 'I envy you. You couldn't care less.' I had never really understood what they meant, or thought; perhaps they didn't know me very well. But they were right. My inward-looking narrow life of climbing and travelling had isolated me. I shared few of the interests or concerns of most other people, and that obviously came across to them in the way I spoke and behaved. For years, my different outlook hadn't bothered me; I relished being an outsider. I liked to travel, to see new and beautiful places and to learn how others lived. My experiences had a profound effect on my thinking. I had lived with constant life-threatening danger in the mountains, seen unimaginable poverty on my travels, and over time had come to consider people's normal day-to-day concerns and worries as petty and trivial. In some ways, I had been right; people in the western world rarely, if ever, have to make life or death decisions, or have to be concerned about where their next meal is coming from. None the less they do have to make serious and difficult decisions that can effect the future well-being of themselves and those around them for years to come. In the end, people's concerns, however small, are real to them, and as such have to be respected.

As time went on, my views became more and more extreme, until I had become isolated and lonely. For months I had been struggling with that reality, and now I realised I had adapted to it. I had changed.

It came to me, as I walked through the streets of that small Chilean town, that I *did* care, not only for myself, but also for those around me. Drifting along in a world of my own was no longer enough. I needed to try harder, to do things better, for myself as well as for others. A few years before, I would probably not have bothered to go and look for Sean; I would simply have laughed at his misadventure and thought no more about it. Rather than a source of hilarity, I now saw it as a cause for concern, perhaps a symptom of some deeper problem or anxiety. My friendship with Sean had a long history – almost ten years. During that time we had variously lived, climbed, worked and travelled together. On several occasions we had spent un-interrupted months in each other's company. Our mutual trust and reliance had extracted us safely from many tight spots over those years. I felt a sense of responsibility towards him.

I paid a visit to the post office and then went to a café to read my letters. I felt in limbo, caught between going home to the world in the letters and the lonely, terrifying world up there on the Central Tower.

A group of Dutch girls came and sat at my table and we fell into a conversation. They had just arrived in Puerto Natales and planned to complete a circular walk around the Towers of Paine. They talked of Tierra Del Fuego, of virgin beech forests and endless tracts of unspoilt wilderness. It all sounded very romantic.

'What have you been doing?' one of the girls asked me.

'I've been climbing,' I announced, too proudly, as if that made my journey somehow more worthy than theirs.

'And have you been successful?'

'Well, not exactly.'

A large tourist poster showing the Towers of Paine hung on the wall, and I was soon on my feet pointing out the features of our climb, tracing the line up the picture. The enthusiasm with which I spoke surprised me. I stopped at our high point.

'And here's where we've got to,' I heard myself saying.

It was so close to the top. I paused and stared into the picture. It was possible to make out exactly where Noel and I had stopped – just above were ledges, patches of snow and broken rock buttresses. The short way from there to the summit looked a lot easier than the climbing we had done already.

'We're going back tomorrow to finish it off,' I said without a trace of doubt in my voice, despite the nagging anxiety that

131

persisted inside me about climbing back up our line of weather-beaten ropes again. Yet the poster showed it clearly – the prize of the summit was ours for the taking. I owed it to myself to try to climb the mountain one final time.

Later I sat in the town square, feeling happier. The sun cast bright summer light on to the trees and flowerbeds. The mountains seemed distant again. It was always the same. The bad memories faded, the joy of movement and sense of freedom remained.

I remembered my first visit to the French Alps – my first time in mountains that would take days rather than hours to climb. Their size, their beauty and complexity stirred my imagination. I had wanted to be among them, picking my way up their steep faces and intricate ridges, to look down rather than up.

The reality had been different. There had always been fear. Avalanches obliterated tracks that I had walked along just minutes before. The silence had been broken by the sickening sound of falling stones. I had watched my ice-axe fall from my grasp and disappear into the darkness in showers of sparks. My body had ached, and I had felt exhaustion as never before. And when the mountain had been climbed, and I had limped back to the valley, the soles of my feet burning with blisters. I had vowed never, ever to return.

Six months later, the pain would have gone. My memories were of horizons studded with peaks and blankets of cloud below; of the sun rising and setting in a blaze of pinks, oranges and mauves; of cold clear nights, when the Milky Way swathed through the sky in a prominent white band – and I made plans to return to the mountains again.

Over time I had learned from my mistakes and my body had become stronger, offsetting the effects of tiredness and exhaustion. I became mentally tougher, shelving bad experiences in the back of my mind at an ever quickening rate. Now, it seemed, I needed only a good meal and a decent night's sleep in order to forget anything I didn't care to remember.

I met up with the others at the supermarket and we bought

food for another week, almost finishing our communal money, making the end of the expedition seem much nearer. My personal money would do no more than get me back to Santiago to catch the flight home.

The evening was a much more subdued affair than the night before. Paul and Sean still had hangovers and Noel seemed preoccupied with his work back in Oxford. Like a group of cowboys in an American Western, we had come into town and basked in the pleasures it offered. Now it was time to return to the country.

'I'm going to give it one more go,' I informed the others over dinner.

'Are you sure, Simes?' Paul asked me with concern in his voice.

'I think so,' I heard myself say.

In the morning we awoke early and joined the tourists waiting for the bus to take us back into the National Park and the mountains.

TEN

State
of
Mind

We arrived back at base camp in wind and rain. After the bright sunny days in Puerto Natales, the good food and the comfort of real beds, it was depressing to return to an austere camp life. Even though we had been absent for only a short time, the place already had a squalid and derelict feel to it.

'Some bastards have been nicking our food,' Paul shouted from the hut. I sprinted across from my tent to see what had been plundered.

'It doesn't look as if they've taken much,' I said after a quick glance round.

Packets of opened food were scattered over the table in puddles of water. Pots and pans lay on the muddy floor. Despite the camp lying off the main tourist trail around the Towers, there had been a steady stream of visitors who usually stayed one night and then left. A party had obviously arrived while we were away in town.

'Well, they could've cleaned up their mess,' Paul grumbled as he started putting food back on the shelves.

The words sounded strange coming from Paul, who was not usually in the least house proud. Although our only claim on the hut was by virtue of taking up residence in it, it had become our home. It felt as if we had been burgled.

The evening passed in tense silence. We all knew that Noel was not going to get another chance to climb the Central Tower. Tomorrow he would have to start the long journey home and we were morosely resigned to the fact.

It was still raining in the morning and, for once, everyone was up early. Noel was already preparing to leave when I entered the hut.

'Have you got everything?' There seemed to be no more to say.

'God, this work business is a bummer,' he mumbled. 'Once I've finished my doctorate, I'm going to take a year or two off and do a lot more climbing.'

For a few minutes we all sat in gloomy contemplation, saying nothing. At last Noel downed the remains of his coffee and stood up.

'Right, I'd better be on my way.'

Paul threw his arms around him and gave him a hug. Then with uncharacteristic formal dignity, Noel shook hands with Sean and me, kissed Hanneke on the cheek and stepped outside. Without hesitating, he picked up his rucsac and walked through the forest out of the camp. After jumping the small stream, he paused and turned to face us.

'Give the mountain your best,' he said. 'See you all back in England.'

He walked away without looking back, leaving us to stare mutely after him. I felt an immediate sense of loss and knew our task would now be harder. We were losing much more than a capable climber. With Noel went a part of our drive and motivation, and at once my doubts returned.

Part of me wished I was leaving as well. We had always taken the climb seriously – we knew all along that it would be difficult and dangerous – but up to now a holiday atmosphere had prevailed. All we had to look forward to at this moment was reaching the top of the mountain merely because we didn't want to face defeat. Why couldn't we be content with what we had done? The climb was beginning to feel like a burden, a commitment from which there was no escape. I was not used to thinking of climbing in this way. I had always done it for enjoyment. There had often been times when it was cold, scary, painful or tiring, but on balance it was always fun. This time the joy had gone.

After breakfast I retired to my tent, bored. There was nothing to do in the camp but wait for the weather to improve, and we had already done enough waiting. I should have been used to it. All mountains have their share of bad weather, but here in Patagonia it was depressing, and there always was the possibility that it would not get better.

I re-read my letters from home, but they gave only temporary relief. It was impossible to ignore the wind, the dripping water and the rhythmic creaking of the tree trunks. All the time I thought of the ropes, strung high up on the mountain. I imagined them swaying wildly in the gusting wind, lashing one way and then the other over the rough rock, and with each movement the fibres parting, weakening the ropes further. Those at the top of the mountain, where the wind would be strongest, were so thin. A sickening fear built up inside me, and I couldn't bring myself to confide in the others in case they were having no such doubts.

The only way to stop my worries was to think of the summit, to imagine struggling up the last few rope-lengths and finally being able to look down in every direction, to see all the fantastic walls and mountains that I knew lay to the north and west, to view the huge mass of the Patagonian ice-cap. Surely that's what mountaineering is all about – to succeed against all the odds, to reach the top? And yet I knew that was not the case. Reaching the summit is only part of a much broader experience. If reaching the top were so important, then all mountaineers would quit with their first failure and move on to another pastime. The trouble was that on this particular mountain reaching the summit had become an obsession. The more I thought about it the more confused I became.

I took a walk in the forest to try to clear my mind. It had little effect. What had seemed so radiant, so full of life, just a few days before when we struggled off the mountain now seemed dull and over-familiar. We had been in Paine over five weeks, and my usual restlessness was returning. I needed a change of scene.

That evening the rain finally stopped. Paul ran excitedly around the clearing.

'This could be our chance, Simes.'

Sean was more reserved.

'Let's wait and see what the weather is like tomorrow. If it's good, we can go up in the evening.'

As it grew dark the sky cleared completely, and the barometer climbed rapidly. When I walked from the hut to my tent a multitude of stars shone from an obsidian sky. All the signs looked good.

I tried to sleep, but felt nervous, excited and more than anything scared. Whatever I did, the image of the thin rope above the bivouac ledge filled my mind. One moment I was jumaring up the rope beneath the icicle-fringed overhang, spinning round in space, the next a violent jerk as the rope parted sent me free-falling into the void below. With over three thousand feet to fall before the collision with the slabs at the bottom, there would be a lot of time in which to think.

I remembered taking a hundred-and-fifty-foot fall down Point Five gully one winter in Scotland. A piece of ice on which I was standing collapsed, my ice-axes ripped out and off I went. At first it had puzzled me – climbing second I should have been held on the rope from above, but I continued to fall. Fortunately the gully was steep which meant I did not smash into anything on the way down, but that also gave me time to think. After the initial shock I rationalised that the belay above must have pulled, and that my partner was following me down the gully. That meant we were going all the way. My thoughts came so quickly and clearly that everything seemed to be happening in slow motion. Facing down like a sky-diver, I watched features go past and the snow slope at the base of the gully coming up to meet me. There was no problem, I reasoned: I would hit the slope quite gently, do a couple of forward rolls, get up and casually brush myself down. My distorted senses told me everything would be fine, and I believed them, even though the reality was quite different. I calmly prepared for the impact.

As it happened, the fall did not go all the way. Suddenly the rope caught me and I was catapulted thirty feet back up the gully, only to fall down again and bounce to a stop. My partner had not fallen with me, but I fell so far because, for some reason, he had not been holding the rope. I was never able to discover why for he was Polish and spoke no English.

Perhaps on that occasion my subconscious mind had been protecting me, sparing me the awful realisation that I was about to die. Maybe falling three thousand feet wouldn't be so bad after all. My mind would protect me, allow me to die in peace. It was a nice theory – one that was easy to live with. But almost as quickly as I constructed it I remembered being at Verdon, a huge limestone gorge in France, when a Belgian soloist had fallen from near the top. I didn't witness his thousand-foot fall to the scree below, but friends told me he had screamed all the way.

Eventually I fell into a light sleep, only to wake once the sun hit the tent. Spells of dozing had done little to relieve my tiredness, although physically I felt strong again.

Everyone was up early. An air of expectancy hung over the camp. Even Hanneke, who had taken no part in the climbing, was excited.

'Will you go up today?' she asked.

'I suppose so,' I replied with flat resignation.

We ate breakfast in silence. I constantly examined Sean's and Paul's faces, hoping to get some idea of what they were thinking. I wondered if they had any doubts or fears. It was impossible to tell. Sean looked tense, but not unusually so. He always took his mountaineering seriously. Paul seemed as cool as ever, sitting calmly with his normal distant gaze. I had already witnessed his casual attitude to danger. In many ways it was enviable, but at the same time I knew some of it came with inexperience. Sean and I had seen mountains kill, had watched avalanches obliterate places that we had considered safe, had seen rock-falls sweep down gullies crossed moments before. With each new experience, and each story told, came a re-evaluation of danger. At times it seemed as if we were beginning to get the measure of the mountains, to be able to pick out danger well in advance and take action to avoid it. Then something unpredictable would happen and make a mockery of our experience. We had seen too much and been around too long to hold the same views as Paul. I wondered if we ever had. Paul was special. Unique.

The day turned out to be good. The sun continued to shine, a small puff of white cloud hovered around the Central Tower and a few strange lenticular clouds remained to the east over the Pampas. From what I had already seen, the weather was as good as you could expect in Patagonia. The conditions for the climb were near perfect, and yet still I did not have a good feeling about it. However much I tried, I could not shake off the image of a breaking rope from my mind.

We took a late lunch and afterwards I went through the careful ritual of changing into my climbing clothes and packing my rucsac, running a list of what I needed repeatedly through my mind. Usually the process was calming, an integral part of my psychological preparation before a big climb. Now it felt like a chore.

As the time to leave approached. I could hear Paul and Sean making their final checks.

'Have you got the barometer?' Sean asked.

'In the top of my rucsac. What about the gas?'

'There's some in my sac and some here for Simon.'

Their voices drifted across my consciousness. Sometimes they were incredibly sharp and at others strangely distant. I felt somehow removed from what was going on. My anxiety surged.

I started to think about how I usually felt before the start of a climb. There had been times when I had hardly given it any thought, when I knew I just wanted to do it without regard to the obvious dangers, or whether I was fit enough. In truth, I had not cared. On such occasions I had not always climbed well, and often found myself out of control in situations (especially when soloing) which could result in a crippling, if not fatal fall. With shaking limbs and fading strength, helped by surging adrenaline, I had battled upwards, slapping for handholds and pedalling with my feet. I had been lucky. At other times in the same mental state all had gone well. Then the experiences had been magical and liberating. With my mind empty, I had been free to enjoy the pleasures of fluid precise movement, as well as my position and everything around me. Climbing then was at its most addictive – and dangerous.

Over many years I have watched others, often very good climbers, become so obsessed with soloing that they do it all the time, to the exclusion of other forms of climbing. Eventually, they carry the same blank stare as war-weary soldiers – as if they no longer care, as if the intensity of the experience has become more important than their own lives. Some step back from the edge by quitting, or by moderating the habit, while others go on to die in accidents.

I have known mountaineers who, flushed with success and ambition, have over-stretched themselves. Like the soloists, there seems to be a sickening momentum leading up to their deaths.

I realised, as never before, that climbing, as with other things in life, should be a matter of balance; that other things were important and interesting, and that I was missing out by neglecting them. If people drink too much, they might well offend and lose their friends, or damage their health. Others who work obsessively may end up ignoring their partners, so leading to a breakdown in relationships. Losing the balance with climbing simply has more serious consequences. Climbers, like people who drink too much or work too hard, are not forced to do it. It is simply a matter of saying no.

'Are you ready to go, Simes?' Paul shouted.

'What?' I called back, even though I had heard the question clearly.

'It's time to go,' Sean stated bluntly.

Without any hesitation I walked over to the hut, where

Paul and Sean were sitting on their rucsacs outside, waiting.

'I'm not going.' I told him flatly.

They both looked deeply shocked, and for a moment there was a tense silence, until an expression of acceptance spread over Paul's face.

'That's all right, Simes,' he said. 'We understand.'

I was not so sure that Sean did. He just stared at me, motionless. I felt awful. The timing of my decision could not have been worse. I was not only letting them both down but making their own mental preparation that much more difficult. It was particularly disappointing for Sean. Our friendship was long-standing and over the years we had come to know and rely on one another.

'I'm sorry,' I said feebly, 'but I just can't face going up again. It does not feel right.'

Sean's expression changed from one of shock to worry. 'I suppose we'd better divide this up,' he said to Paul, pointing to the piles of food and gas on the ground.

I felt relieved; relieved that I was not going up, that Paul and Sean had taken it well, and that they had not made it difficult for me by trying to persuade me to change my mind. I could only hope that my decision had not affected their own motivation too badly.

'I think I need another brew,' Paul announced.

'I'll get you both one,' I said. 'It's the least I can do.'

Later, as we all sat drinking in the hut, I let out a few of my fears.

'Be very careful going up the ropes, especially the thin one above the bivouac ledge.'

'We will,' Sean assured me. 'We could take up another rope from the portaledges to protect ourselves on that top section.'

'Yeah, not a bad idea,' Paul said thoughtfully.

When both their drinks were finished, Paul and Sean looked at one another for a moment, before standing up and walking outside. Hanneke and I followed them out.

'Take care,' I said as they lifted their rucsacs on to their backs.

'Good luck,' added Hanneke.

'See you in a couple of days,' said Sean, holding out his hand.

I shook it and immediately felt happier. Then he turned and left the camp, closely followed by Paul.

'Climb the bastard,' I shouted as they disappeared up the path.

Highs
and
Lows

For a while Sean and Paul walked quickly, heads down, up the steep twisting path above the camp. Their mood was sombre and neither spoke. At a point where the path crossed the small stream it followed up the hillside, they stopped to drink. As they took it in turns to catch handfuls of water Sean broke the tense silence.

'I'm worried,' he said.

'Why's that?'

'Climbing as a pair is going to be much more serious. Don't you see that?'

'Well, yeah, I suppose so.'

'If either of us has an accident and injures himself, it will be virtually impossible for the other to get him down.'

'I hadn't really thought of it like that.'

'Well, perhaps you should,' Sean said bluntly. 'Then there's that thin rope above the bivouac ledge. If we get into trouble up there we really will get stuffed.'

'But we've already talked about this,' Paul said defensively. 'We can make it safe by belaying each other.'

'It would be a lot safer with three of us.'

'Oh, come on, Sean. I'm sure it will be all right,' Paul pleaded.

'Let's just hope so,' Sean said, picking up his rucsac and continuing up the path.

Meanwhile, I stood and stared at the empty path long after Paul and Sean had gone out of sight, unable to take in what had happened. What were they thinking or saying about me? I half expected them to return and announce that they too were not going up.

'I'll go and put the kettle on,' Hanneke said, snapping me from my day-dream. It was some time before I followed her back into the hut.

'Are you all right?' she asked as I sat down next to the fire.

'I suppose so.'

I slumped forward and rested my head in my hands. The hut was completely still when eventually I looked up.

'I feel awful for letting them down, but I just didn't feel right about going back up again. When we came down from the last attempt, I told myself that was it, there was no way I was going up again. But after a day in town I convinced myself that I could manage one final push. It was only while we were preparing to leave that I realised I'd been kidding myself. My heart's just not in it any more.' I paused for a moment before adding. 'Perhaps I didn't drink enough in Puerto Natales.'

This was dreadful. Not content with letting Paul and Sean down, I was now pouring out all my doubts and confusions on to Hanneke. She appeared to understand.

'I think you made a brave decision,' she said.

I didn't feel brave at all. It seemed to me more like cowardly self-pity.

'Maybe I've been on too many climbing expeditions over the last few years and just need a break from them.'

'Could be.'

I was glad Hanneke was there. I felt more comfortable talking to her about such things than with any of the others. She was an outsider. I could say what I wanted to her without wondering if she would take it the wrong way, or if it would upset the status quo in the group. Above all, Hanneke offered an opinion without being judgemental.

I remembered returning from my last climbing expedition during which my ankle had been badly sprained in a fall. It happened high on Pobeda – the largest mountain in the Tien Shan range in Kazakhstan – and although in a serious position, our Russian hosts had managed to get me down the mountain safely. Later, back in England, I had been surprised to find myself utterly exhausted, both mentally and physically. It took the enforced inactivity while recovering to realise that I had allowed myself to become run down. Only six months before I had returned home after nine months in Asia on three successive expeditions, and in the two years before that I had been away travelling and climbing continuously for a year and a half. Now, none of it seemed to have any purpose.

When questioned by others, I had often justified my punishing schedule by pointing to a need to challenge myself, to learn from the different experiences travel brought, and to escape from what I saw as the normal dull routine of day-to-day living. This, I often argued, gave me a clearer perspective on life and put everyday fears and anxieties into context. I had ridiculed people caught up, as I saw it, in a mindless pursuit of wealth. Because I had been doing something different, I had not seen the parallel in my own life. Well, climbing and travelling were no longer an escape but an obsession just as mindless as pursuing money for its own sake. They had simply become a different form of consumerism. Now the obsession had run its course, and I understood that it had been responsible for my feelings of isolation and loneliness over recent months. The knowledge was little comfort in my present state of distress.

That night I went to bed early but found it difficult to sleep. No matter how I tried to dismiss the thoughts that continuously circulated in my mind, I still felt guilty about letting the others down, and worried about their safety.

*

Fit from weeks of continual exercise, Paul and Sean made swift progress up the path and were soon under the Towers. They paused briefly to fit crampons to their boots at the foot of the glacier. The storm had stripped most of the remaining snow from the surface, exposing permanent hard blue ice underneath, criss-crossed with narrow crevasses. At first the going was easy, but as they got higher up the glacier the crevasses became wider and deeper, forcing detours along their edges, to where they were narrow enough to jump, or to natural bridges of ice that offered a way across.

At the base of the slabs a gap had opened up between rock and glacier so that the start of the ropes was out of reach, forcing a further detour. Paul crossed on to the rock some way from the rope and delicately traversed across to reach it, hastily clipping himself on and throwing the rope across the chasm to Sean.

Once secured to the rope their confidence began to return. They quickly built up rhythm and momentum, moving up the slabs at the bottom of the face. The slabs were now completely free of snow, making the traverse along the diagonal line of the ropes less treacherous than it had been before. The sound of avalanches was now replaced by that of running water which percolated from the rock in small rivulets. The storm had finally freed the mountain from the grip of winter.

Paul swarmed up the ropes, leaving Sean to follow at his usual steady pace. When he reached the portaledge camp, Paul looked at his watch; it was eight in the evening, so they were making good time.

Rummaging through one of the haul-bags, he recovered the hanging stove and set it up. The ledge was now virtually free of snow, forcing him to melt pieces of dirt-stained ice hacked out from under the portaledges. The melted ice produced an un-appetising soupy liquid with gravel in the bottom, which Paul eagerly gulped down before topping the pan up with more ice.

Sean arrived breathing heavily, hot and flustered from the steep section of climbing under the portaledge camp. Sweat ran down his forehead and dripped from the end of his nose.

'You okay?' Paul asked.

'I've felt better and I've felt worse,' Sean replied in his usual non-committal way. 'I'm still worried though.'

'I'm sure it'll be okay. Look at the weather.'

'How long have we got here?' Sean asked with a sigh.

'A few hours. Last time Noel and I left here around midnight, to join you at the top bivouac.'

'Well, that's a relief,' Sean said, collapsing into the sitting position on the narrow ledge.

Paul kept the stove going, constantly making drinks, finding it more and more difficult to refill the pan with ice. Between bouts of eating and drinking they sat in silence, just the pair of them alone on the huge granite wall, gazing out at the land below, lost in their own thoughts.

'I think we should get moving again,' Paul said, as the final light of the day faded and the air developed a chill. It was already past eleven o'clock. They would have no trouble climbing in the dark as they were simply following the ropes already fixed in place. By the time they reached the top of the lines and were ready to move above them, it would be light again.

When the rucsacs had been packed and Paul swung out on to the rope soaring above the portaledge camp, the first stars were already shining from a dull mauve sky.

Urged on by the cold night air, Paul moved swiftly up the rope, soon regaining his jumaring rhythm and warmth. At the first changeover he turned on his headtorch as Sean started up the rope below. As the darkness intensified, their worlds became defined by the small pools of light cast by their torches. The rope disappeared above and below, seemingly suspended from nothing. Only when reaching belays, with their clusters of shiny karabiners and bunches of knots, were they reminded of what the rope was hanging from.

Through the night they made their way steadily upwards, occasionally stopping to rest. Before long the aches and pains that had vanished while in Puerto Natales returned as harnesses cut into their waists and stopped the blood from flowing freely to their legs. Within an hour of dawn Paul realised he was nearing the bivouac ledge and increased his pace, knowing that he could soon have a break. Feeling a huge sense of relief he finally pulled on to the ledge and paced around to get the blood flowing round his aching legs. He felt very tired. Fearing the cold, he scrambled into his sleeping bag and moments later was asleep.

Just as it was starting to get light, Sean wearily hauled himself on the ledge.

'Paul!' he shouted on seeing the outstretched sleeping bag. 'What about a brew?'

After a few muffled moans, Paul emerged from the bag and began rummaging in his rucsac for the stove.

*

When I awoke, my first thoughts were for the pair of them up there, I lay churning over their imagined progress in my mind. They should be above the top bivouac, possibly at the top of the ropes, but I knew no more at the end of my spell of idle speculating than I did before.

Outside it looked like a perfect summit day, renewing my doubts about choosing not to go up. A jealous part of me momentarily wished the weather had turned for the worst, so vindicating my decision, but it quickly passed, giving way to more positive thoughts. More than anything I wanted them to succeed, to finish what we had come to do. Then we could all happily go our separate ways and move on to something new.

Later, inside the hut, Hanneke and I lingered over breakfast. The atmosphere was nowhere near as intense as when the others were in the camp. It was pleasant just to relax and chat. Compared to the rest of us, Hanneke seemed so humane. During the expedition she had happily taken a back seat and in her own quiet and undemonstrative way had encouraged and supported us in what we were doing. To me, it seemed as if she was contributing a lot more to the expedition than she could possibly be getting out of it.

'Will they reach the top today?' she asked.

'They should do, but you can never be sure,' I replied, wishing I could share her enthusiasm.

'Isn't it exciting?'

To Hanneke, each experience was fresh and new, something

to be savoured and enjoyed. For me it had become a routine. She had worked for a year and a half to save the money to come to South America, and it obviously made her experience that much more rewarding, while all I had done in recent years was to escape from life's normal responsibilities.

I remembered days wandering along perfect white sandy beaches fringed with palm trees in India, standing at the side of the road while trying to hitch a lift in the Australian out-back, driving a motor-bike along jungle tracks in Thailand and endless horizons of mountains with fondness but without longing. Those years had been reckless, carefree and mad. I had been lucky and privileged to have such experiences, and I regretted none of it, but I had reached a point where it was no longer satisfying. Looking back, I could see that in many ways I had been fortunate to survive. I had never truthfully considered my own mortality before – just lived for the moment. The future had simply been the next climbing trip. Perhaps I had not expected to live, or even not wanted to live. Now I could see life stretching away in front of me. There could be no doubt about it, I would have to make adjustments and settle down to some planning.

During the day, I collected wood for the fire, took short walks in the forest and occasionally went to the clearing by the river to look up at the Towers, hoping in some way it would help to protect Paul and Sean. I expected to see them, but the cap of cloud swirling round the summit never lifted, so I fell back on imagining where they were.

In the evening we cooked a large meal and afterwards sat by the fire, drinking pisco.

'What will you do when you get back home?' Hanneke asked.

'I don't know exactly,' I said hesitantly, taking another swig of the liquor. If I want to I could go on an expedition to Nanga Parbat. It's one of the harder Himalayan 8,000-metre peaks.' My voice carried little conviction.

Hanneke looked puzzled. 'That doesn't sound to me like the answer,' she said perceptively.

*

Paul and Sean lay impatiently on the bivouac ledge, waiting for the stove to produce hot water. The process was slow and annoying. Gradually the sun crept above the Pampas, bathing the top of the Central Tower in weak golden light and warming the chill morning air. Far below, the glaciers and valleys were still locked in deep shade. The dawn made them anxious, aware that valuable climbing time was already being lost. Paul willed the stove to work faster, but the monotonous purring sound stayed the same. Now and then, he shook the gas bottle and briefly the flame would flare, producing a high-pitched roar before quickly returning to normal. They both hoped that drinks would lessen the feeling of tiredness.

After two cups of strong coffee neither felt revived. Sleeping still seemed the most natural way to spend the day, but they wanted to finish the climb as quickly as possible while the weather held.

'Come on, we'd better get going.'

Sean stood up and started to pack away his kit. Paul led off up the thin rope fixed above the camp. Neither mentioned arranging a belay with the spare rope; it no longer seemed important. They would take their chances. The storm had done little damage to the thin rope at the overhang and it held. When Paul reached the high point, he tied himself on, sorted out the remaining equipment and looked at the way ahead. The wind had increased and thin cloud now bubbled around him.

The climbing immediately above did not look easy. The crack in the steep slab led up into a snowy gully which steepened to another overhang that was split by a line of iced-up cracks at the top. He could not see what lay above that and silently hoped it would be the last major difficulty.

When Sean arrived, Paul moved on above the belay, following the crack until it ended, still short of the gully.

'Watch me here!' Paul yelled down as he unclipped from the last pieces of equipment and started to traverse left on a line of tiny handholds.

Sean braced himself as Paul executed the difficult moves which became progressively harder as he approached the gully. Several times he slipped and looked as if he was off the rock, but each time he somehow managed to regain his balance. On the final moves into the gully he had to chip away ice from each handhold before he could use it. With pedalling feet, he lunged into the gully, and for a moment appeared to be on the verge of falling, but he found some holds and steadied himself.

At first, Paul was able to move swiftly up the easy-angled gully by kicking steps into the snow, but it soon became steeper and the covering of snow petered out. Above, ice-choked cracks led up to and through the overhang. He reverted to artificial climbing, painstakingly clearing the cracks of ice with his peg hammer to allow equipment to be placed in them. Slowly and carefully, he moved up from one piece of equipment to another. He began to struggle as the crack grew thinner and shallower, so that each gear placement became worse than the last. Anything he tried to insert ripped out on being given a testing tug. Only after several attempts did Paul finally get something to hold before moving with utmost caution up again. Sean watched anxiously from below.

Then, just as he approached the lip of the overhang, he fell. Sean clenched the rope tightly as Paul's body somersaulted down, accompanied by the metallic rattle of equipment hitting rock and high-pitched twangs from the rope as piece after piece of gear ripped from the crack. For a moment, Sean thought his companion was going to fall on top of him, but instead he hit the snow in the gully with a dull thump and went into a roll before jerking to a halt as a piece of gear in the bottom of the crack held firm.

Paul lay winded in the snow, struggling to take in lungfuls of air. He peered down at Sean.

'I'm okay. Sorry about that. I'll go back up in a minute,' he gasped before slumping back into the snow in a fit of panting.

A few minutes later he monkeyed up the rope and carefully climbed back to his high point. This time he made no mistakes and cleared the lip of the overhang, letting out a huge scream as he went over the top and prepared a belay. Sean mistook the significance of the scream until he had jumared frantically up the rope to join Paul on a small ledge. Above was a shallow-angled snow slope, broken by small rock buttresses.

'It looks like we've cracked it,' he said as Sean joined him on the ledge. 'Can you see those ropes above?'

'Yes. You know whose those are, don't you?'

About a hundred feet above them a rope hung from the first rock buttress, it could only have been left by a team of Germans who had climbed another route on the face the year before.

'Give me the kit,' Sean demanded.

Moments later he raced up the snow slope, pausing to rest every twenty feet or so. At the base of the first rock buttress he made a belay, and Paul followed him up. They both sensed that the summit was near, and for the first time knew they would reach it. But there was no room for complacency. Paul had taken a long time to lead the first difficult pitch and the day was passing.

Paul led off up the pitch above, reaching the German rope and using it to surmount the rock buttress. Above that the rope frustratingly disappeared into the snow. Paul had hoped it would go uninterrupted to the top, and once more he was forced to do without it. He ploughed up the next patch of snow and scrambled over the next shattered buttress, hauling himself up small sections of frayed and abandoned rope. Soon they were swapping leads again. As they gained height, so the wind increased. Clouds hurtled by engulfing them in swirling mist, only to clear suddenly, revealing patches of bright blue sky above.

At the next belay the wind was much stronger. Dimly in the cloud above they could just make out the shadowy outline of a jagged ridge. Sean pointed and let out a strangled yelp of delight. It had to be the top. After weeks battling up the east side of the mountain, they would soon get their reward by being able to look to the west. Paul led off and was soon moving more easily over broken rock, following the now continuous line of German rope.

The rope ended at a clump of metal pegs just below the ridge. Paul pushed his head up over the top and reeled backwards. There was no further to go, and the full force of the wind blowing from the west hit him. He braced himself and tried again. With watering eyes, he gazed down the other side of the mountain through momentary breaks in the cloud. Across the valley the huge granite walls of the Fortress and the Shield were clearly visible. Beyond the mountains, far out to the west, the massive expanse of the Southern Patagonian Ice Cap filled the horizon.

A few minutes later Sean was beside him, receiving Paul's bear hug before he had a chance to poke his head over the other side. Paul took out his camera and, holding it at arm's length, pointed it towards themselves and pressed the shutter release. He gestured to a small tower of rock about thirty feet to the left. They grinned at one another mischievously. On a calm day it would be an easy climb, but today the howling wind prevented it. Not that it mattered. They had reached the top of the Central Tower of Paine; the slightly higher summit seemed an irrelevance.

In the biting wind, they soon started to feel very cold. Sean pointed to his watch. It was already six o'clock. With one last glance over the bleak landscape to the west, as if to be assured they'd really made it, they set to work making anchors for the first abseil, and within minutes Paul slid off down the ropes. When they had both reached the end of the rope, Sean tried to pull it down while Paul prepared another anchor. The rope would not budge.

'Give me a hand here,' he shouted above the screaming wind.

Even with the pair of them hanging on, the rope would not move. It was caught somewhere above.

'It's no good,' Sean said finally. 'I'll have to go back up and free it.'

As he jumared back up the rope, Paul waited, anxiously checking his watch every few minutes as he became thoroughly chilled. It was vital they got back to the ledge and their sleeping bags before nightfall. So high up on the mountain in ever strengthening winds, the temperature would plummet and make them dangerously cold. When Sean finally returned, he had done his job well and they were able to pull the rope down, but they had wasted valuable time.

On the following abseils, they were more careful, checking as they slid down that the rope ran in a line free from obstructions that might snag it as they pulled it down behind them. Below, the process was even more complicated as they started to take down the rope fixed in place. Time slipped by and darkness fell.

It was almost midnight when Paul finally reached the bivouac. He slumped to his knees, exhausted, hungry and dehydrated, but he knew it was vital to get on with melting snow to replenish the fluids they had lost during the day if they were not to feel worse in the morning. After shedding his climbing equipment and his boots, he slid into his sleeping bag, intending to get comfortable before starting the stove. Moments later he was asleep.

Sean cursed when he arrived on the ledge and found Paul in a state of oblivion. There was little point in waking him. He filled a pan with snow and lit the stove, fighting off the desire to sleep as he patiently waited for the water to boil. When hot drinks were made, he woke Paul, who gratefully gulped at the mug of liquid before falling unconscious again. In a dream-like state, Sean refilled the pan with snow and continued the long, lonely vigil far into the night.

*

I slept well that night and in the morning lay awake only briefly in my tent, with a dull light filtering through the fabric. Outside I found the sky overcast and cloud obscuring the top third of the Central Tower. As I made my way over to the hut Hanneke emerged from her tent.

'Not such a nice day,' she remarked.

'I'm worried about the others.'

'Where will they be now?'

'Well, if everything has gone to plan, they should be on their way down. They might even be at the portaledge camp.'

'Oh good, then they should be down here soon.' Hanneke said with an optimism that I found hard to share.

'Let's hope so.'

As the morning passed, so the wind increased. It started to spit with rain. Several times I went to the clearing in the forest, hoping to see Paul and Sean making their way down the path. I did not like this role of waiting, nor the feeling of helplessness.

After lunch, a pair of climbers arrived and set up camp next to the top hut, the only one we had not been using. One of the pair wandered down to introduce himself.

'Hello, I am Michel Piola,' he said.

'Hi. I'm Simon, this is Hanneke. Would you like a brew?'

I recognised the name immediately. Michel was a well-known Swiss climber who had completed many new routes in the Alps, as well as some in the Karakoram and Patagonia. For a while we chatted idly. I handed him a cup of coffee.

'We have come to try a line on the east face of the South Tower.' He paused. 'And you?'

'The east face of the Central Tower.'

'And how far have you got?'

'It's finished. My two friends are coming down from the summit today,' I said with pride. The Swiss man looked thoughtful.

'Is that the route started by the Gallego brothers?' he asked.

'Yes, that's right.'

'They did not telephone you?'

'No.' I was puzzled by his questioning. 'Why do you ask?'

'Just a few days before I left Switzerland they telephoned me and asked me not to climb this route on the Central Tower. They also called a group of Italian climbers who were coming here and asked them not to go up it.'

'Do you mean the Gallego brothers are coming here to climb the route we have just finished?'

'Yes, in a few days' time. I believe.'

I felt a wave of joy welling up inside me, and although I managed to hold back my laughter, I still felt a broad grin spread across my face.

'Well,' I said, 'they're going to be disappointed.'

In the afternoon six Italians arrived. They were very friendly and asked politely if they could use the hut in which Noel had been sleeping as their kitchen. To my surprise, in a few hours they had demolished the hut to its foundations and rebuilt it. They had even brought along a huge box of tools and a roll of plastic for the purpose.

'How come we weren't that organised?' Hanneke asked with a laugh.

'Well, we bagged the Gallegos' route.' I said gleefully. 'What more did you want?'

By the evening there was still no sign of either Paul or Sean. The weather was as bad as the worst of previous storms and I began to feel deeply anxious, convincing myself that something dreadful must have happened. I found myself becoming irritable and snappy as we ate our evening meal. Hanneke did her best to console me, but I left half of my food and snatched my jacket off a hook above the fire.

'If they're not down by morning, I'll go up and look for them,' I said to her brusquely as I left the hut to go to my tent.

TWELVE

∾

Down
to
Earth

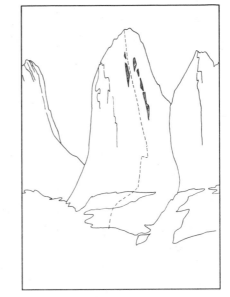

'Paul! Paul! Wake up. We've overslept.' Sean shook the lumpy sleeping bag beside him and banged the water pan with his spoon.

Paul woke with a startled jerk, sat up and peered out while still inside the hood of his bag.

'Oh, hell!' he groaned, instantly recognising their precarious position.

They were surrounded in cloud, the wind was howling and the fabric of their sleeping bags and coils of rope were flapping wildly.

Still feeling exhausted, they got up at once and started packing their rucsacs. As soon as they were ready to leave, Sean fixed the first abseil belay and dropped the ends of the ropes over the edge. Instantly they blew up in the air and lashed around.

'It's no good,' he shouted. 'You'll have to abseil with them.'

Paul pulled the ropes back and tied a knot in the ends which he then clipped to his harness, coiling the rest over his shoulders. Cautiously he began to lower himself, uncoiling the ropes as he went. Sean waited anxiously on the ledge for the weight to come off the ropes, allowing him to follow. In order to leave the mountain clean, he would have to take down the fixed line

157

as he went, painstakingly coiling it to keep it out of the way of the abseil ropes. The whole process was going to be very slow.

At the first belay it took their combined strength to pull the ropes down against the force of the wind. Abseil followed abseil, hour after hour, with the thunderous gusts of wind pounding them relentlessly. The further down they went, the more fixed rope they accumulated, until the weight became an unbearable burden. Eventually Sean decided they could carry no more.

'Right!' he shouted. 'I'm going to get rid of some of this.'

Unclipping a coil from the belay, he hurled about three-hundred feet of rope into the void below. The coils hovered momentarily in the air before shooting upwards in the massive updraught and disappearing into the cloud. Sean was terrified.

Further down, Paul grew impatient waiting for Sean and made two abseils on his own down the fixed rope to the small ledge on the wall above the Coffin. Up above, Sean struggled alone to drag down the abseil rope, becoming more and more frustrated and angry at being abandoned. Eventually he managed to free it, but it had taken a long, lonely time.

'What the fuck do you think you're playing at?' he shrieked at Paul when he reached the ledge.

'I'm sorry,' Paul mumbled, but it did little to appease Sean's anger.

'You could have got me killed!'

'I made a mistake. I'm sorry.'

'Okay,' Sean said, struggling to calm down. 'But from now on we stay together. Right?'

Paul nodded his head and let out a long breath. Both were now dangerously tired, too tired to go back up the rope to help if the other got into any difficulties higher up.

They slid down rope after rope in a wind-numbed daze, each draped in increasingly heavy coils of rope which made controlling their descenders difficult.

Paul was first to reach the portaledge camp as the light began to fade. He crouched and waited for Sean, who abseiled down the overhanging wall above in a series of pendulums, the gusting wind blowing him first one way, then the other. At the bottom of the abseil he struggled to pull himself on to the ledge and could only manage to crawl along on all fours to join Paul.

'I'm absolutely shattered,' Sean yelled above the wind noise. 'I say we leave all the rope and portaledges here and zip down the ropes to the glacier.'

'I'm not going to argue,' said Paul, visibly shaking with cold and fatigue. 'We can come back up another day and clear the bottom section of the mountain.'

'Come on then. Let's get out of here,' said Sean, getting to his feet.

They both longed for the ordeal to end, to be back in camp, out of the wind and out of danger. More than anything, they wanted to stop now, to lie down in their sleeping bags and go to sleep, but they knew if they did that it would be the finish of them.

As they raced down the lower slabs, they counted the abseils with a feeling of anticipation, knowing that with each one they were a little closer to safety. It was dark by the time they crossed the bergschrund on to the glacier. Out on the open glacier the wind hit them with its full force, making them fight every inch of the way. For a while they were reduced to crawling. Even then they were forced to lie flat as the strongest gusts tore into them.

Once off the glacier, they staggered down the path like drunkards, tripping over, crashing into boulders and taking bruising falls. Once or twice the wind took their feet from under them, dumping them heavily on the ground, but it no longer mattered, they no longer cared. The mountain had been climbed and they were safe. When they stumbled noisily into camp in the middle of the night, completely drained and almost incoherent, neither was in any mood for celebration.

'I'll see you in the morning,' Sean said, dumping his rucsac in the small lean-to at the side of the hut before staggering off to his tent. I vaguely remember hearing a disturbance but, failing to connect it with their return, didn't get up.

Paul went inside the hut and lit a candle. For a while he

scoured the shelves for food, his mind still racing, but he soon found the empty cold hut uncomfortable and made his way to his tent.

*

The tent shook violently around me, and for a moment I thought I was back on the portaledge up on the Central Tower.

'Simon! Simon!' A voice shouted outside the tent, adding to my confusion as I tried to shake off the night's sleep. 'They're back! They've done it!' Hanneke called, the excitement in her voice now unmistakable.

I felt a brief pang of envy, but it was overwhelmed by a profound sense of relief. At last it was all over and they were off the mountain safely.

'I'm coming!' I shouted, rushing to get my clothes on.

As I ran across to the hut, still zipping up my jacket, the depression that had plagued my time in the mountains finally lifted. At long last all our dreams and efforts had amounted to something. For once the mountains had been just.

Paul, sitting on a log outside the hut, smiled as I approached. Although he had had the benefit of some sleep, he looked desperately tired, the gaze from his sunken blue eyes still distant. He stood up stiffly and we threw our arms round one another.

'Well done,' I said into his ear.

'You should have come, Simes. It was beautiful up there.'

'Was it difficult?' I asked.

'Well, it was no picnic. Coming down yesterday was a nightmare.'

'I'm not surprised. You didn't pick a good day for it.'

The storm had passed, the cloud was breaking up and shafts of sunlight were making their way into the forest.

'Where's Sean?' I asked.

Paul pointed to the hut and I opened the door to see Sean crouched over a pan in the fire.

'Congratulations,' I said, holding out my hand.

We shook hands, went into an embrace and slapped each other's backs. For a few moments I was stuck for words.

'I'm glad you're back, I wasn't looking forward to going up to look for you,' I said. 'Have you seen the new arrivals?'

'Yeah, it does seem to have got busy while we've been away.'

'By the look of it, we've finished just in time.'

'Not quite,' Sean said. 'We've got to go back up to the portaledges and bring them down. The rope as well.'

'Yes, but that won't take long. A day at the most.'

'True,' said Sean, 'but we're going to need a rest first.'

'So, you'll be going back up after a brew and a bite to eat?' I teased.

'I thought you would go up and do it for us,' Sean replied.

'No thanks,' I said firmly. 'I've got an important appointment in Puerto Natales with some glasses of beer. I don't suppose you'd be interested, would you?'

'I just might take you up on that,' Sean said, smiling.

*

Later, I sat for a while thinking of what might have been. I could have gone with them and reached the summit. Others might say I had blown a wonderful opportunity by being too cautious and taking the wrong decision. Yet it had been just one, in a series of crucial decisions spanning the whole expedition. Deciding to come here in the first place had been the simple part. In many ways the climbing itself had not been so very difficult – we were very competent climbers after all. Then why had I given up, opted out instead of completing what we had come here to do? Suddenly I realised it was all a matter of looking after yourself, both mentally and physically, of keeping yourself in a condition that would enable you to climb effectively and not make mistakes. In the end, it boiled down to small, almost minute-by-minute decisions that might not seem important at the time but which could have detrimental effects several hours or even days later – simple things, like not drinking or eating enough, not putting a jacket on, or forgetting to take just one piece of equipment.

Similarly, in everyday life people might consider getting married, having children, starting a business or buying a house as the biggest decisions they will ever make, but the success of each of these ventures depends on the multitude of decisions they make later, not the move to undertake the venture in the first place.

I recalled one of the most serious decisions I have ever had to make when, high on a mountain in Peru, I had chosen to cut the rope on which my partner, Joe Simpson, was hanging with an injured leg. Alone, I struggled to hold him as he swung on the rope one hundred and fifty feet below me. Sitting without anchors in a collapsing stance on an open snow slope that was threatening to avalanche, I found my position becoming increasingly desperate. Slowly but surely I was being pulled off the mountain. Eventually I would fall.

Some would argue that there was no decision to be made; that cutting the rope and the powerful symbol of trust and friendship it represents should never have entered my mind. Others say that it was simply a matter of survival, something I was forced to do.

As it happened, for a long time I simply hung on, hoping that Joe would be able to take his weight off the rope and relieve my position. By the time I remembered I had a knife in the top of my rucsac I was at the end of my tether, unable to hold him for much longer. I knew I had done all that could reasonably be expected of me to save Joe, and now both our lives were being threatened. I had reached a point where I had to look after myself. Although I knew my action might result in his death, I took the decision intuitively in a split second. It simply felt the right thing to do, like so many critical decisions I had taken during the climb. Without hesitation, I removed the knife from the rucsac and cut the rope.

Such moments of intuition always seem to feel the same – impersonal, as if the decision has not come from my own mind. Only with hindsight could I see there had been a build-up to that moment. During the days before, we had made many errors of judgement. We had not eaten or drunk enough and carried on climbing long after nightfall. By doing so, we had allowed ourselves to become cold, exhausted and dehydrated.

162

One evening I became so cold waiting outside for Joe to finish digging a snow hole that some of my fingers became frostbitten. In short, we had not looked after ourselves.

It was no doubt exhaustion that caused Joe to make a mistake descending a small ice cliff soon after starting down from the summit, to fall and break his leg. I had then taken on the job of getting him down the rest of the mountainside, lowering him rope length after rope length, in great personal danger due to the lack of anchors. During that nightmare descent I made further errors. Even though it was growing dark, I decided that it would be better to reach the bottom of the face before stopping for the night. As we got lower, visibility poor in the cloud and swirling snowstorm, I failed to compensate for lowering him in a straight line when we needed to be moving diagonally to avoid the huge ice cliff over which he ended up hanging.

It was impossible to see what happened but I felt the sudden wrench on my harness. Before long I was unable to take Joe's weight from the belaying device on my waistband and thus free another hundred-and-fifty feet of rope that was prevented from passing through by a knot joining it to the stretch of rope on which Joe hung. That extra rope would have allowed me to lower him further, and it might have prevented what followed.

As it was, after cutting the rope I spent a torturous night in a snow hole dug into the slope, convinced that my actions had resulted in Joe's death. The next morning I started the treacherous climb down to the base of the ice cliff, firmly believing I would die trying to make it back to the camp.

I managed to skirt round the ice cliff and descend to the side of it, only to discover, to my horror, that at the bottom was a deep crevasse twenty feet across and almost a hundred yards long, into which Joe must have plunged after the rope was severed. The sight vindicated my dread, and although I shouted, I was not surprised when there was no reply. It seemed inconceivable that anyone could have survived such a fall.

Stricken with fear and remorse, I continued my descent alone. Eventually I made it off the glacier, but gained little comfort from the knowledge that I was going to survive. The guilt still remained. For a long time, as I staggered down the moraine back to camp, I wondered how to break the news of Joe's death. I even considered inventing a story to make it easier for myself. But when, just above the camp, I met our friend Richard Hawking coming up to look for us, tearfully I blurted out exactly what had happened.

While Richard was sympathetic and not in the least judgemental, I spent the next few days in a state of acute anguish, guilt and shock, trying to recover in the camp before setting out for home, Unknown to either of us, another nightmare of epic proportions was being played out further up the valley.

It never occurred to us that Joe might not have been killed by his fall into the crevasse. Still less did we imagine him landing on a precarious snow bridge deep inside it. No one who has not read *Touching the Void,* Joe's account of the terror and agony he suffered extricating himself from the dark depths of that cavern of ice, could guess what he went through before beginning his three-day crawl down the glacier and across the moraine, without food and with very little water.

When in camp Richard and I heard howling in the night, we went out with torches to investigate and found Joe a hundred yards away lying on some boulders in the darkness. At first I could not believe what I was seeing. It was as if I were witnessing some sort of sick supernatural joke. Then, almost at once, I was flooded with confused emotions; relief and joy that Joe was alive; shock and sorrow at the state he was in and the pain and suffering he had been through; guilt that my actions had left him abandoned on the mountain.

Later, inside the tent, Joe thanked me for all my hard work trying to get him down. He told me that he did not blame me for cutting the rope, that he would have done the same in the circumstances. Those words were a great comfort to me. They allowed me to put a line under the affair and push it to the back of my mind almost there and then. The whole experience had been so bizarre anyway that it seemed like a fairy story, and now it had a happy ending.

All my agonising after cutting the rope had not changed

anything. My decision had been right; we had both survived. In subsequent years, I have overheard numerous heated debates about the ethics of my decision and many 'what if' scenarios. I have met people who are understanding of my actions and others who are openly hostile. Their secondhand opinions mean nothing compared to the words Joe uttered to me in the tent that night in Peru. With the greater mountaineering skills and experience I now possess, I do not believe that I would get into such a situation again, but if somehow I did, I know that my decision would be the same. In just one respect I feel I was neglectful. In the extreme stress of my predicament I came to the conclusion without a close inspection that any attempt at rescue in the crevasse was impossible. On reflection, I can see that it would probably have done more harm than good to have tried, but it simply did not occur to me to go to the edge and look carefully into the depths.

Ultimately, we all have to look after ourselves, whether on mountains or in day to day life. In my view that is not a licence to be selfish, for only by taking good care of ourselves are we able to help others. Away from the mountains, in the complexity of everyday life, the price of neglecting this responsibility might be a marriage breaking down, a disruptive child, a business failing or a house repossessed. In the mountains the penalty for neglect can often be death.

Paul and Sean had decided to go back up the mountain, and were rewarded by climbing to the summit. To them, the margins of safety seemed acceptable. I still considered what they had done to be dangerous, but then mountaineering is risky – that is one of its attractions. At its limits, the line between a safe decision and a reckless one is very fine. I have come to believe it is always best to be honest and simply to follow our hearts. We will not always be able to stop the agonising afterwards, but perhaps we should pay less attention to it. That agonising is useful only if we have worked out a false or wrong scenario that does needless injury to others for our own advantage.

I had seen in a moment of intuition that I was not calm or confident enough to be capable of seeing exactly what needed to be done minute by minute if I went back up the Central Tower. In such a state I would put not only myself but the others in grave danger. Rather than go with Paul and Sean, I chose to stay in the camp and so could justly feel at ease with myself. As in Peru, I could draw a line under all the self-examination, push the events to the back of my mind and look forward to something new.

*

'Hey, what are you going to call the route?' I asked Paul as we dragged branches from the undergrowth back to the camp for firewood.

'I thought El Regalo de Mowama would be a good name.'

'Yeah? What does it mean?' I was impressed by the speed at which Paul had been picking up Spanish.

'It means the gift of Mowama. The Tuelche Indians believed the god Mowama lived up among the Towers.'

'Well, it's a nice name. Did I tell you the Gallego brothers are on their way here to climb our route?'

'You're kidding! How do you know?'

'Piola told me they'd phoned him and the Italians to warn them off.'

Paul sniggered. 'O-ho! Could that mean trouble, do you reckon?'

'I think I'll be on my way tomorrow and leave you to it,' I said. 'What are you going to do next?'

'Sean's keen to make a circuit of the Towers and take some photographs. Then maybe we'll do some more climbing before seeing if we can catch the boat up to Puerto Montt.'

'I'd be tempted to join you if I had the money,' I said, suddenly anxious about the uncertain future awaiting me at home.

It sounded a much more enjoyable option than returning to Britain in the middle of the winter and trying to find work. For a moment I considered the possibility. I felt sure that one of them could be persuaded to lend me the money to stay another month or so, but it was too easy. This time I was determined to break the pattern. I would go straight home and face up to the responsibilities that I had run away from in the past. Having decided that the life of a climbing nomad was no longer for me, I had to break the cycle.

'What about you?' Paul asked.

'Go back to Sheffield and look for a job, I guess. I just hope I can get one quickly.'

My words came out with no enthusiasm. Paul looked at me as if he had just learned that I had contracted a terminal illness.

'I'm sure it'll work out for you,' he said. 'Are you interested in coming back to Patagonia next year, maybe to Fitzroy?'

'I don't know,' I said hesitantly, immediately wondering how wise it would be to make such a commitment after deciding to take a firmer control of my life at home and give it some positive direction. Still, it was a year away. There was plenty of time to get my life sorted out. 'Same team?' I asked.

'Yes.'

'Well, this trip's been successful. I'd certainly be interested.'

'Good. Well, that's settled then,' said Paul, his face brimming with eagerness. 'It'll be great, Simes. There's loads to climb, we'll just have to find a good objective.'

Paul was off again. I felt a growing sense of alarm, but it seemed a shame to interrupt his fantasies. I let his flow of dreams drift across my consciousness until finally they dried up.

'I think there's still some pisco back in the hut,' I said. 'Fancy a drink?'

'Why not?'

We dumped the branches outside the hut, gave Sean and Hanneke a call and went inside to find the bottle. There was not enough for a real celebration. Hanneke came into the hut clutching a small flat stone.

'I've made something for you,' she said, handing the stone to Paul. He examined it carefully with an expression of awe, before handing it to Sean.

'It's beautiful,' he said. 'Thanks a lot.'

I watched, fascinated, wondering whatever could be so interesting and beautiful about a stone until it was passed to me.

Hanneke had painted a picture of the Central Tower on the side and marked our route up the mountain with a series of black dashes. She had even added our names, as well as the one Paul had chosen for the route.

'I thought it could hang with all the others,' she said, pointing to the line of wooden plaques hanging on the wall next to the wooden telephone.

The plaques were a record of other climbers who had used the hut and the routes they had climbed during their stay. Sean found a piece of wire, wrapped it round the stone and used the ends to hang it next to the others.

'Perfect,' he said, standing back to admire his handiwork. 'We should have an artist on all our expeditions.'

The following day the weather was perfect – the sort of day that gives you the feeling it's going to be fine for weeks on end. I packed my bags under the clear blue sky, the sunlight burning my skin. Perhaps we had come too early, I thought. As we walked away from the camp I felt none of the anxiety and frustration that had hounded us down the valley and into the town after the first attempt on the summit. The expedition was now complete, and we were leaving rather than fleeing. Having done what we set out to do, all the tensions and stresses were gone. We ambled down the path like a group of friends on holiday, chatting happily, enjoying each other's company.

Down at the Estancia, Pepe greeted us with a broad smile and brought out a crate of beer from his hut when he heard of Paul and Sean's success. Later, we helped Pepe and his family to make a huge fire out in the open and spent a wonderful evening lying in the long grass around the fire, talking quietly, gazing into the flames as the hills turned golden under the setting sun. As it grew dark we ate a simple meal of sausages, cooked on the embers, with platefuls of fresh salad.

'I have to go into town soon,' Pepe said. 'I could drive you all in my jeep tomorrow if you like.'

'Okay,' said Sean, 'but you must let us take you and your family out for a meal – as a thank you for all the help you've given us.'

In the morning we started early, loaded up the jeep and set off along the rough track over the foothills to the road. The day was perfect again, and the Towers looked surreal. Already the memories of the giddy drops, the sweeps of granite, the boiling clouds and the howling wind were fading. It was hard to believe we had been up there among them. It felt as if the previous weeks had been no more than an elaborate dream.

Just before the track reached the road to Puerto Natales, Pepe stopped the jeep at the side of a river. I remembered wading across it with our bags when we first arrived. Now it was swollen with meltwater and had burst its banks. Pepe stood at the side examining where the track entered the water. It was a good two hundred yards to the other side, and although the grey cloudy water looked sluggish, it was obviously deep.

I had just resigned myself to carrying all our kit over the small footbridge further downstream and waiting for the bus when Pepe jumped back into the jeep and rammed it into gear.

'Hold on!' he shouted.

Moments later we were in the water, which rose quickly above the wheel arches. The engine began to labour, and then we were floating. Water poured into the well under the front seats as we drifted downstream. The jeep did not make a very good boat, and for a moment I thought it was going to capsize, but soon we had crossed the deepest section of water and the wheels started to grip the river-bed again. Pepe drove triumphantly up on to the other bank and we all started to laugh nervously.

'I thought we were going to drown then,' I said. 'After all we've been through . . .'

'Tell me about it,' Sean said drily.

Pepe waited a short time for the water to drain out of the vehicle before driving on to the gravel road heading for Puerto Natales. I gazed back towards the Towers through the swirling dust, watching them grow ever smaller, until we crested a hill at the end of Laguna Amarga and they disappeared from view.

Near a group of houses a little further along the road a party of climbers stood at the side next to a large pile of kit-bags.

'Look, it's the Spanish contingent!' Paul shouted as we sped past. We waved and jeered at them as they cowered in the dust kicked up by the jeep.

The evening in Puerto Natales was rather sombre. Paul and Sean were still tired and I could find little reason to celebrate my return to England. It felt as if we were just going through the motions. Before we parted I thanked Pepe for his help and promised to look him up if I ever came back again. As we walked back to the hosteria, I couldn't help thinking the night had been an anti-climax.

'You don't fancy the Miladon Disco tonight then?' I asked casually.

'Not tonight,' Sean and Paul said in a loud chorus.

In the morning the others helped me with my bags to the bus stop. We waited in a nearby café, staring silently into cups of coffee, feeling more and more uncomfortable.

Eventually the bus arrived and the driver disappeared round the side of the café. Some while later, he reappeared, climbed into the cab and started the engine. We ran for the door in a fumble of people and luggage and my bags were stowed in the back luggage hold. I hugged Paul and Sean, kissed Hanneke on the cheek, and climbed aboard. The impatient driver barely let the last passenger on before closing the door and driving off down the street, leaving the three sad figures waving feebly on the pavement.

Later, I changed buses in Punta Arenas and settled down for the long journey northwards across the Pampas. The same video was being shown on the bus as on the journey down all those weeks ago. The view out of the windows was equally monotonous. The man in the next seat introduced himself as a Greek political journalist.

'I think politics is dead,' he lamented. 'What is your work?'

'I do a lot of mountaineering,' I explained.

He looked out of the window and then stared at me as if I had lost my mind. Outside was one of the flattest places on earth. The bus cruised steadily across the Pampas, towards Santiago and the challenges that I had avoided for far too long at home.

Epilogue

In the months that passed after my return from Patagonia I watched my remaining money dwindle before being offered a job as an access technician in London. The job hardly lived up to its rather grand title, amounting to little more than routine maintenance to the outside of tower blocks. What made it different was that the work entailed abseiling down the buildings on ropes. It was physical, dirty, monotonous and not without an element of danger, but at least it paid well and was outside in the open air. I was even promised more work in the future. Compared with mountaineering, it was easy. I bought a car with some of the money I earned and felt pleased with the independence it gave me. Previously I had always hitch-hiked.

*

A calmness came over me as the suburbs of London finally gave way to open countryside. The trees looked radiant in their fresh summer leaves and fields of wheat and barley shimmered in the breeze. Small white clouds tracked across the bright blue sky, casting shadows on the land below. I calculated it had been twelve years since I had spent an entire summer in England. I had forgotten how beautiful it was.

I met Noel in Oxford, and Hanneke and Steve who had come over to England on holiday from the States. We drank and talked in the pub where we had made the final preparations in the hectic days before the expedition. Now we had come full circle and could laugh at our memories. It all seemed such a long time ago. Hanneke, happy and relaxed, told me how she was enjoying her new life in America.

On my way home to Sheffield I took another detour to visit my parents in Leicestershire. Driving through sleepy little villages and past my old school, I wondered why I had ever gone away. I remembered my first explorations in the fields around my parents' house and the constant yearning to find new territory and experience the adventures it would provide. The search had taken me further and further from home, and when I was older I was able to extend my explorations on a bicycle. I could see clearly that climbing and travelling were just a natural extension of what I had always done.

Suddenly I was lost. The back lanes along which I had cycled as a teenager were no longer familiar. I sat at a junction trying to remember the village names on the signpost. It seemed ironic that my urge to explore had taken me away from all that I once knew and those whom I loved. I could see that, for a while, I had gone too far, and in the process had forgotten what I had learned of who I was and where I came from.

Further up the motorway I turned off at Chesterfield and drove into the Peak District, eventually parking my car at the bottom of Stanage Edge. It was late. Climbers were already making their way down the path from the crag. I took out a small rucsac and raced up the hillside.

At the bottom of the crag I paused to take off my shoes and put on climbing boots. Moments later I was climbing, fumbling to tie my chalk bag round my waist as eagerly I made the first few moves. The rock felt perfect to the touch, both dry and warm, without the greasiness that develops after rain or a particularly warm day. I loved such evenings and moved swiftly up the rock, feeling lighter with each move. The top came so quickly that I skipped down a grassy gully between two buttresses and started another climb. From time to time I stopped to gaze out across the rolling golden moors and the deep-cut valleys cast in shadow. On such evenings I knew that I could never give up climbing.

At the top two youths who were wandering across the moor approached me.

'Do you know where Robin Hood's Caves are, mate?' one asked.

'If you follow the top of the crag along for about four hundred yards, they're down on your left. You'll find them at the back of a platform about two-thirds of the way up the cliff,' I said, pointing across the rolling heather.

'Oh, cheers,' he said before they wandered off, still looking lost.

I thought nothing more of the request until I got nearer the caves and heard noises. A steady stream of people were making their way along the top towards them as a loud and haunting sound rolled across the crag. Sticking out from the front of the caves was a long brass horn, like those used by Tibetan monks. A red-headed girl stood at the other end, blowing into it. The sickly sweet smell of marijuana wafted by in the breeze. Suddenly it was obvious what was happening. I was missing out on a midsummer's day party.

In that brief moment the changes in my life seemed clear. I had begun to take responsibility for myself at home as well as in the mountains. Just a year or two before, without knowing how or why, I would have been up there in the caves with the revellers. I would simply have gone with the flow and followed the crowd without stopping to think if it was what I really wanted. Life had seemed too short to worry about such things.

Now I felt calmer. I had slowed the pace of my life enough to be able to think clearly, to take control of what I was doing. There now seemed to be so many interesting things to do as well as climbing, and enough time in which to do them all. Although my future was uncertain, and no doubt a multitude of difficult decisions lay ahead, I could accommodate it all. I knew the mountains would remain a consuming passion, but I had learned to put them in perspective, and to look after myself at home as well as when among them.

Acknowledgements

By far my greatest debt of gratitude belongs to my companions on the trip – Noel Craine, Paul Pritchard, Sean Smith and Hanneke Steenmetz. After all it is their story I have told as much as mine. I would also like to thank them for their continued support and help while I was writing the book, and for providing photographs for it.

In Chile we met many wonderful and kind people. In particular, I would like to thank Pepe Marusic and his family for their hospitality and help getting in and out of the mountains, and also Steve Hayward for his advice and loan of a rope.

Big wall climbing is a very equipment-intensive sport. We would have been unable to start such a climb without generous donations of kit from Buffalo Clothing, DMM Ltd, Hugh Banner, J Rat, Karrimor International Ltd, Lyon Equipment and Rab Down Equipment. Mountaineering expeditions can also be expensive, and for the Central Tower climb I must acknowledge our debt to the British Mountaineering Council and the Mount Everest Foundation for their financial assistance.

On a more personal note, I would like to thank my mother for writing to me in Chile and on all my other travels; Joanne Raybould for helping me through a difficult patch in my life around the time of the expedition; Jane Murray for her love and support while I was writing this book; Jackie Simpson for her maps and drawings that appear in the book; my editor at Cape, Tony Colwell, for his incredible patience; and my family and friends for their unflagging encouragement.

Finally, I must express my gratitude to Joe Simpson for telling my side of the Siula Grande story so faithfully and truly in his book *Touching the Void.*